Success in Math
Consumer Math

Student Edition

GLOBE FEARON
Pearson Learning Group

Executive Editor: Barbara Levadi
Market Manager: Sandra Hutchison
Senior Editor: Francie Holder
Editors: Karen Bernhaut, Douglas Falk, Amy Jolin
Editorial Assistant: Kris Shepos-Salvatore
Editorial Consultant: Harriet Slonim
Production Manager: Penny Gibson
Production Editor: Walt Niedner
Interior Design: The Wheetley Company
Electronic Page Production: The Wheetley Company
Cover Design: Pat Smythe

ISBN 0-835-91184-5

Printed in the United States of America

7 8 9 10 11   06 05 04 03

1-800-321-3106
www.pearsonlearning.com

Contents

Chapter 1 Earning Money   **1**
   1•1 Keeping Track of Part-Time Wages   2
   1•2 Deducting Job-Related Expenses from Earnings   4
   1•3 Figuring Hourly Wages and Overtime   8
   1•4 Keeping a Weekly Time Card   12
   1•5 Working with Hourly Rates and Tips   14
   1•6 Computing a Salary From Information Given in   16
       a Want Ad
       Review   20
       Practice Test   22

Chapter 2 Take-Home Pay   **23**
   2•1 Understanding Earnings Statements   24
   2•2 Calculating Deductions   26
   2•3 Calculating Take-Home Pay   28
   2•4 Understanding Tax Forms   30
   2•5 Filling Out Tax Forms   32
       Review   36
       Practice Test   38

Chapter 3 Budgeting   **39**
   3•1 Finding Average Monthly Expenses   40
   3•2 Average Fixed and Variable Expenses   44
   3•3 Making a Monthly Budget   46
   3•4 Using a Budget   48
   3•5 Adjusting a Budget   50
       Review   52
       Practice Test   54

Chapter 4 Personal Banking   **55**
   4•1 Managing a Checking Account   56
   4•2 Reconciling a Bank Statement   60
   4•3 Using a Savings Account   64
   4•4 Finding Simple Interest   66
   4•5 Finding Compound Interest   68
   4•6 Borrowing Money   72
   4•7 Comparing Loan Repayment Plans   74
       Review   76
       Practice Test   78

Chapter 5 Becoming an Informed Shopper   **79**
   5•1 Recognizing Hidden Costs   80
   5•2 Understanding Discounts and Sales   82
   5•3 Shopping from Catalogs   86
   5•4 Reading Advertisements   90
       Review   94
       Practice Test   96

Chapter 6 Making a Purchase   97

   6•1 Understanding and Calculating Sales Tax   98
   6•2 Estimating and Calculating Change   102
   6•3 Installment Buying   106
   6•4 Using Bank Credit Cards and Charge Accounts   110
   6•5 Reviewing Credit Plans   112
      Review   114
      Practice Test   116

Chapter 7 Buying Food   117

   7•1 Using Nutrition Labels   118
   7•2 Using Unit Pricing to Compare Costs   120
   7•3 Using Coupons   122
   7•4 Preparing Meals   124
      Review   126
      Practice Test   128

Chapter 8 Transportation   129

   8•1 Using Public Transportation   130
   8•2 Calculating Commuting Costs   132
   8•3 Buying an Automobile   136
   8•4 Insuring and Maintaining a Car   140
      Review   144
      Practice Test   146

Chapter 9 Housing   147

   9•1 Finding Affordable Housing   148
   9•2 Calculating the Cost of Utilities   150
   9•3 Signing a Lease   152
   9•4 Painting and Carpeting Your Home   154
   9•5 Calculating Fixed Monthly Home Expenses   158
      Review   162
      Practice Test   164

Glossary/Index   165

Selected Answers   171

Chapter 1
Earning Money

OBJECTIVES:

In this chapter, you will learn

- *To calculate total part-time wages before taxes and deductions*
- *To calculate earnings after paying job-related expenses*
- *To calculate weekly earnings*
- *To use a time card to find the total number of hours worked*
- *To calculate total weekly earnings, including tips*
- *To calculate hourly, weekly, monthly, and yearly salaries*

When you look for a job, what questions should you ask? Here are some suggestions:

What training do you need to do the job? How much does the job pay? How many days must you work? How many hours must you work each day?

This chart shows information about some jobs.

Job	Hours per Day	Days per Week	Salary
Cashier	5	3	$7.30 per hour
Data Entry	8	5	$18,750 per year
Hairdresser	7	3	$250 per week + tips
Waiter/Waitress	8	5	$275 per week + tips
Auto Mechanic	8	5	$1,975 per month
Store Clerk	4	4	$6.75 per hour

Which job pays the most, not including tips? Compare the hairdresser's job to the waiter/waitress's job. Which job pays more, including tips of about $25 per day?

In this chapter, you will learn how to find the answer to these and other questions about earning money.

◢1•1 Keeping Track of Part-Time Wages

◢ **IN THIS LESSON, YOU WILL LEARN**

To calculate total part-time wages before taxes and deductions

WORDS TO LEARN

Part-time job *a job that requires fewer working hours than a full-time work week*

Wages *the amount of money a worker earns in a given time period*

Suppose you work at a health club after school and on Saturday. This chart shows how much you earned last week. How can the manager find the total amount she must pay you for the week?

Work Day	Mon.	Tues.	Wed.	Thurs.	Fri.	Sat.	Sun.	Weekly Wages
Your wages	$12.50	$20	$14.75	–	–	$21.45	–	?

New Idea

You have a **part-time job** (pahrt tyem jahb). This means that you work fewer hours than a full work week. The money you earn is called your **wages** (WAYJ-uhz).

The manager can find your total weekly wages by adding the amounts you earned each day. To check herself, she can estimate the total before she adds. To estimate, if the cents amount is $.49 or less, round down to the last dollar. So, $21.45 becomes $21.00. If the cents amount is $.50 or more, round up to the next dollar. Then, $14.75 becomes $15.00.

Estimate your total weekly wages. Round each amount. Then add.
13 + 20 + 15 + 21 = 69
The estimated total is $69.

Find the exact amount of your total weekly wages. Using paper and pencil, write the exact amounts in a column, lining up the decimal points. If you have a calculator, enter each digit and decimal point. Then to add, press ⊞ after each entry. Press ⊟ to get the total.

12.50 ⊞ 20.00 ⊞ 14.75 ⊞ 21.45 ⊟ 68.7

The exact total is $68.70.

Focus on the Idea

*To find total weekly wages, write the amounts earned each day in a column, lining up the decimal points. Then add. Using a calculator, enter each digit and decimal point. Press the ▇**+** between entries. Press ▇**=** to get your total.*

Practice

This chart shows how much part-time workers earned last week at P.J.'s Supermarket. Find each worker's weekly wage. Then answer exercises 4 to 7. The first one is done for you.

	Workers	Mon.	Tues.	Wed.	Thurs.	Fri.	Sat.	Weekly Wages
1.	Larry	$13.50	$14.50	–	$21.00	–	$12.25	$61.25
2.	Rita	$11.50	$17.75	–	$21.00	–	$15.75	_____
3.	Jerome	$13.25	$15.50	–	$16.75	–	$15.75	_____

4. How much did Rita earn on Monday and Tuesday?

_____

5. Compare Rita's wages with Jerome's wages.

   a. Who earned more by the end of the week? _____

   b. How much more? _____

6. At the end of the week, Jerome received a paycheck for $58.75.

   a. Is the amount of his check correct? _____

   b. If not, how much more or less should he have received?

   _____

Apply the Idea

7. Suppose you are the manager of P.J.'s. Estimate whether $300 is enough to pay the part-time workers for last week.

_____

✎ Write About It

8. Your take-home pay last week is shown. Explain how you could estimate how many weeks you need to work to buy a jacket for $97.75.

Monday	Tuesday	Thursday
$13.75	$15.20	$18.40

_____

_____

1•2 Deducting Job-Related Expenses from Earnings

Ms. Harris has been hired as one of the first female firefighters in her town. She will be paid $620 a week. She will have expenses that she must pay in connection with her job. Some of these expenses are:

Dinners	$35.00 per week
Transportation to and from work	$21.25 per week
Uniform-cleaning bill	$7.25 per week

How much will Ms. Harris earn each week after paying her job-related expenses?

New Idea

Ms. Harris is paid a salary for her work. Her **salary** (SAL-uh-ree) is the amount of money paid to her by her employer for work she performs. Her salary is sometimes called her wages, or **earnings**. (ERN-ihngz). But Ms. Harris has expenses that she must pay in connection with her job. These are called **job-related expenses** (jahb ree-LAYT-ihd ehk-SPEHNS-uhz).

To find how much money Ms. Harris has left each week after she pays her job-related expenses, here are the steps to take.

Find the total amount of Ms. Harris's weekly expenses.

Step 1   Add to find her total weekly job-related expenses.

$$\begin{array}{r} \$ \ 35.00 \\ 21.25 \\ + \ \ 7.25 \\ \hline \$ \ 63.50 \end{array}$$

Step 2   Subtract her weekly expenses from her weekly salary.

$$\begin{array}{r} \$620.00 \\ - \ 63.50 \\ \hline \$556.50 \end{array}$$

Ms. Harris has $556.50 left after paying her job-related expenses.

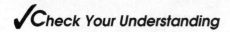

1. Why does Ms. Harris subtract her job-related expenses rather than add them to her salary?

_____

_____

Focus on the Idea

To find the amount of salary, or earnings, that remains after job-related expenses have been paid, subtract the total expenses from the salary.

Practice

Find the worker's earnings after job-related expenses have been paid. The first one has been started for you.

2.
Weekly Salary	Weekly Expenses	
$375.00	$ 15.75	Lunch
	+ 10.50	Transportation

Total Weekly Expenses: _$26.25_

Earnings After Expenses: _____

3.
Monthly Salary	Monthly Expenses	
$1,500.00	$ 82.50	Lunch
	15.00	Uniform rental
	+ 48.80	Transportation

Total Monthly Expenses: _____

Earnings After Expenses: _____

Extend the Idea

Before you subtract job-related expenses from your salary, be sure that salary and expenses are for the same period of time. If your salary is paid weekly, your expenses must be calculated weekly.

Example: Suppose you work three days a week and earn $175 a week. If you pay $2.75 a day for meals and $3.75 a day for transportation, how much of your salary is left after you pay job-related expenses?

Because your salary is paid by the week and your expenses are listed for a day, you must change your daily expenses to weekly expenses. Because you work three days a week, find your expenses for three days.

Find the total expenses per week.

For meals: $3 \times \$2.75 = \$8.25$

For transportation: $3 \times \$3.75 = \$11.25$

Total weekly expenses: $\$8.25 + \$11.25 = \$19.50$

Now, subtract your total weekly expenses from your salary.

$$\$175.00 - \$19.50 = \$155.50$$

After you pay job-related expenses, $155.50 of your earnings remains.

✓Check the Math

4. Suppose you have a friend whose only job-related expense is for transportation. He pays $2.75 for train fare twice a day. His salary is $475 for a five-day work week. Your friend says he can calculate how much of his salary is left after he pays his expenses by multiplying $2.75 by two and subtracting that product from $475.

   a. Is he correct? (Hint: Is he calculating salary and paying expenses for the same period of time?)

   _____

   b. How much of your friend's salary is left per week after he pays his job-related expenses?

   _____

Practice

Solve each problem. The first one is done for you.

5. Each week, Maurice has job-related expenses of $12.50 for transportation, $13.75 for lunches, and $12.75 for insurance. What are Maurice's total weekly job-related expenses?
   _$39.00_

6. Avra earns $275 on her part-time job. Her expenses are $17.50, $15.38, and $6.10. How much of her total salary is left after paying her job-related expenses? _____

Find the amount of each salary left after job-related expenses are paid.

7. Salary: $350.00 per week. Job-related expenses: $32.75 per week. _____

8. Salary: $1,750.00 per month. Job-related expenses: $101.75 per month. _____

9. Salary: $31,177.00 per year. Job-related expenses: $127.50 per month. _____

10. Salary: $450.55 per month. Job-related expenses: $25.50 per week. _____

Apply the Idea

11. Suppose you need a job that will pay enough so that you will have at least $125 a week left after you pay job-related expenses. A job at a local restaurant pays $150 a week for a three-day work week. It will cost you $4.25 each day for transportation and $2.50 each week to clean your uniform.

    a. Would you still earn at least $125 per week?

    _____

    b. Show how you found your answer.

    _____

12. Abraham's salary is $225 per week. His job-related expenses include $15.75 per week for transportation and $12.50 per week for meals. Chandra's salary is the same as Abraham's. She works three days a week and pays $3.50 per day for transportation and $5.25 per day for meals.

    a. After paying weekly expenses, does Abraham or Chandra have the greater amount of salary left?

    _____

    b. Show how you found your answer.

    _____

✎ Write About It

13. Use a newspaper to find a want ad for a job that lists a salary. Write down what your job-related expenses might be for that job. Calculate how much of your salary you would have left after expenses. Explain why you would or would not apply for the job.

    _____

    _____

    _____

    _____

    _____

◢1•3 Figuring Hourly Wages and Overtime

⬛ IN THIS LESSON, YOU WILL LEARN

To calculate weekly earnings based on hourly rate of pay and overtime pay

WORDS TO LEARN

Full-time job *a job that requires from 35 to 40 hours of work each week*

Hourly wage *amount paid for each hour of work*

Overtime *number of hours worked beyond a regular full-time work week*

Suppose you have just been offered a job that requires you to work a full-time work week. You are told that you will be paid by the hour. You will work the same number of hours each week. What do you need to know in order to compute your weekly salary?

New Idea

If you have a **full-time job** (fool tyem jahb), you must work a full work week, usually from 35 to 40 hours. To find your weekly salary, multiply your **hourly wage** (OWR-lee wayj), or the amount you earn for each hour of work, by the number of hours you work in one week.

Example: Suppose you find out that you will have to work a 35-hour week. You will be paid $16.50 per hour. What will your weekly salary be?

Find your salary using pencil and paper.

$$\begin{array}{r} \$16.50 \\ \times\ 35 \\ \hline 8250 \\ 4950 \\ \hline \$577.50 \end{array}$$

Find your salary using a calculator. Enter each digit and decimal point. Enter ☒ after 16.50 and ▣ after 35.

16.50 ☒ 35 ▣ 577.5

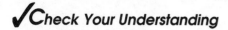

1. Suppose that a year has passed and you get a raise. You now earn $18.50 per hour.

    a. Explain how to calculate your weekly salary.

    _____

    b. What is your new weekly salary?

    _____

    Focus on the Idea

    To find a weekly salary when you are paid by the hour, multiply the hourly wage by the number of hours worked.

Practice

Here is a chart showing hourly wages and hours worked per week for four people. Find the weekly salary for each person. Then, complete the chart. The first one has been done for you.

	Worker	Hourly Wage	Hours (Week)	Salary
2.	Tamara	$7.25	40	$7.25 × 40 = $290.00
3.	Leon	$12.00	37	_____
4.	Bill	$26.75	39	_____
5.	Iola	$19.75	35	_____

Extend the Idea

Suppose that one week you must work 8 hours **overtime** (OH-ver-teyem), or 8 more hours than your usual full-time 35-hour work week. Your work rules say that overtime pay is one-and-one-half ($1\frac{1}{2}$) times the regular hourly rate of $18.50, or "time and a half."

To find out how much you would earn:

Step 1   Find your weekly salary:

$18.50   Per hour
× 35   Hours
$647.50   Weekly salary

Step 2   Find your overtime rate of pay.

Use the decimal 1.5 for $1\frac{1}{2}$:

$18.50   Per hour
× 1.5
$27.75   Overtime rate

Step 3 Find your overtime pay.

$27.75   Overtime rate/hour
   × 8   Hours
$222.00   Overtime pay

Step 4 Now, add the amount of your overtime pay to your weekly salary.

$ 647.50
+ 222.00
$ 869.50   Total earnings for the week

✓Check the Math

6. LeRoy earns $10.20 per hour for the first 40 hours he works. He gets paid two times his regular hourly wage, or "double time," for each hour of overtime. He worked 4 hours overtime last week and expects to receive an extra $102 in his paycheck for overtime.

   a. Is he correct? _____

   b. Explain your answer.

   _____

   _____

Practice

Complete the chart. Find the total salary. The first one has been done for you.

	Hourly Wage	Hours (Week)	Weekly Salary	Overtime Rate	Overtime Hours	Total Salary
7.	$18.50	40	$740	1.5	6	$906.50
8.	$12.25	38	_____	2	7	_____
9.	$11.75	35	_____	1.5	10	_____
10.	$9.25	35	_____	2	15	_____

Solve.

11. Mark earns $9.50 per hour. How much will he earn per hour of overtime if he is paid 1.5 times his regular hourly rate?

   _____

12. Ina earns $13.50 per hour. How much is her weekly salary if she works 36 hours per week? _____

13. Lara earns $12.00 an hour for a 40-hour work week. She gets 1.75 of her regular rate for overtime. How much will she earn if she works 46 hours in one week? _____

Apply The Idea

14. Workers at a local assembly plant earn $8.50 per hour for a 40-hour work week. The overtime pay rate for weekdays is time and a half. The overtime pay rate for Sundays and holidays is double time.

    a. Jose worked 44 hours last week, including 4 hours on Sunday. How much did he earn? _____

    b. How much will Jose earn if he works 48 hours with four hours on Sunday? _____

Use this chart for exercises 15 and 16.

Job	Hourly Rate	Hours (week)	Overtime Rate
Nurse's Aide	$6.80	36	1.5
Store Clerk	$6.00	40	1.8

15. In which job would a worker earn more for a full-time week with no overtime? Show how you can tell.

_____

_____

16. Which job would pay more for working a 50-hour week? Explain and show how you found your answer.

_____

_____

✎ Write About It

17. Explain why some overtime pay is called "time and a half."

_____

_____

_____

_____

◄1•4 Keeping a Weekly Time Card

Time Card

Name: Jill Ruiz   **Hourly Rate:** $8.25   **Job:** Cashier

Week of: 1/3 – 1/10

DAY	DATE	TIME IN	TIME OUT	LUNCH/ DINNER	TOTAL HOURS
Mon.	1/3	8:00 A.M.	5:00 P.M.	1 h	?
Wed.	1/5	1:00 P.M.	4:30 P.M.	–	?
Fri.	1/7	9:00 P.M.	4:00 A.M.	1 h	?

How can Jill figure out how many hours she has worked each day?

New Idea

Jill's **time card** (tyem kahrd) records the time Jill begins and ends work each day.

On Monday, Jill started work at 8:00 A.M. and ended at 5:00 P.M. She does not get paid for the hour she took for lunch. Jill counts to find the number of hours she worked in the morning. From 8:00 A.M. to 12:00 noon is 4 hours. Jill then counts from 12:00 noon to 5:00 P.M. (5 hours). She adds the morning and afternoon hours (9 hours) and subtracts an hour for lunch. Jill worked a total of 8 hours.

On Wednesday, Jill worked only in the afternoon. She subtracts her starting time from her ending time.

On Friday, Jill determines her number of hours just as she did for Monday.

Focus on the Idea
To use a time card to find total number of hours worked, count hours until noon or midnight, then count hours after noon or midnight.

Practice

Use the time card to find the total hours worked each day. The first one has been done for you.

Time Card					
Name: Frank Jones		**Hourly Rate:** $6.25		**Job:** Gas Station Attendant	
Week of: 4/8 – 4/14					
DAY	DATE	TIME IN	TIME OUT	LUNCH/ DINNER	TOTAL HOURS
1. Tue.	4/8	2:00 A.M.	10:00 A.M.	1 h	<u>7 h</u>
2. Fri.	4/11	9:00 P.M.	4:00 A.M.	1 h	_____

3. Show how to find the total hours Frank worked on Friday.

_____

4. Did you figure Frank's Friday hours in relation to noon? Why or why not?

_____

Find the number of hours that pass.

5. From 8:15 A.M. to 7:30 P.M. _____

6. From 9:00 A.M. to 5:45 P.M. _____

7. From 1:45 P.M. to 6:15 P.M. _____

8. From 5:15 A.M. to 11:30 A.M. _____

Apply the Idea

9. Carrie earns $7.75 per hour. She worked Monday, Tuesday, Wednesday, and Thursday from 4:30 P.M. to 1:00 A.M. with a one-hour dinner break each day. How much did she earn for the four days of work? _____

Write About It

10. Ask four students who have a part-time job whether they use a time card at work. Ask students who do not use a time card how they keep a record of the number of hours they work. Report on the results you find.

_____

_____

_____

_____

1•5 Working with Hourly Rates and Tips

In This Lesson, You Will Learn

To calculate total weekly earnings, including tips

Words to Learn

Employer *a person who hires and pays workers*

Employees *people who work for someone in return for wages or salary*

Suppose you could work at a fast-food restaurant where you would be paid a salary. Or, you could work at a coffee shop and be paid less in salary but also earn tips. Which job would you choose? Why?

New Idea

You probably would choose the job that paid more money. So, the answer to the question depends on the amount of each hourly wage and the amount earned in tips. An **employer** (ehm-PLOY-uhr) is someone who hires and pays **employees** (ehm-PLOY-eez), or the people who work for wages. Employers usually pay a lower hourly wage for a job where part of an employee's income comes from tips.

Suppose the fast-food restaurant pays $6.25 per hour and the coffee shop pays $4.50 per hour. However, the employees at the coffee shop usually earn $45 in tips in an eight-hour workday. To find an employee's total earnings, add the daily wage and the tips.

Fast Food Restaurant		**Coffee Shop**	
$ 6.25	Hourly	$4.50	Hourly wage
× 8	Hours	× 8	Hours
$50.00	Daily wage	$ 36.00	Daily wage
		+ 45.00	Tips
		$ 81.00	Total earnings per day

You would earn more money at the coffee shop, which pays a lower hourly wage but includes tips.

Focus on the Idea

To find total earnings, including tips, add the amount of tips to the wages.

Practice

Solve.

1. Suppose you know a worker's hourly wage and the number of hours she works in a week. You also know how much money she earns in tips. What do you do to find the worker's total weekly earnings? Write the letter of the correct steps.

   _____

   a. multiply hourly wage by tips; add number of hours
   b. add tips to hourly wage; multiply by number of hours
   c. multiply hourly wage by number of hours; add tips

Find each employee's weekly salary and total weekly earnings.

	Employee	Hourly Rate	Hours Worked	Weekly Salary	Tips	Earnings
2.	Mira	$5.30	24	_____	$245.00	_____
3.	Marco	$5.76	32	_____	–	_____
4.	Ivana	$9.25	45	_____	–	_____
5.	Ben	$7.90	30	_____	$448.00	_____

Apply the Idea

Peter earns $6.75 per hour. He works 36 hours per week. Two weeks ago he made $75.50 in tips. Last week he made $88.75 in tips.

6. What were Peter's total earnings two weeks ago?

   _____

7. How much more were Peter's total weekly earnings last week than two weeks ago? _____

Write About It

Suppose you knew only this information about two jobs:

   Supermarket checker: $8.50 hourly wage

   Limousine driver: $6.50 hourly wage plus tips

8. Write about which job you would prefer and why. Tell what other information you would like to know about the job you prefer.

   _____

   _____

   _____

◢ 1•6 Computing a Salary from Information Given in a Want Ad

▼ IN THIS LESSON, YOU WILL LEARN

To calculate hourly, weekly, monthly, and yearly salaries based on information in want ads

WORDS TO LEARN

Apply *to make a request in writing or in person*

Help Wanted
PART-TIME SALES CLERK
The Best Sporting Goods
$7.25 an hour
3 days a week
5 hours per day
Apply in person.

Position Available
SERVICE STATION ATTENDANT
Samco Gas Station
3 days a week
5 hours per day
$110.25 per week
Apply in person.

The jobs listed above were advertised in the classified advertisement section of a newspaper. How can you tell which job pays the greater salary?

New Idea

To **apply** (uh-PLY) for a job, you request, or ask for the job in person, by mail, or by fax. Before you apply for one of these jobs, you probably want to know which salary is greater. The sales clerk job tells the amount of the salary per hour. The gas attendant's job lists a weekly salary. To compare any two salaries, both must be expressed in terms of the same unit of time, such as per hour, per week, or per year.

To begin, find the attendant's hourly rate. Find out how many hours per week the attendant must work.

$$
\begin{array}{r}
5 \text{ Hours per day} \\
\underline{\times\, 3} \text{ Days per week} \\
15 \text{ Hours per week}
\end{array}
$$

Use this information to find the attendant's hourly rate.

$110.25 ÷ 15 Hours = $7.35 Per hour

Now you can compare hourly rates for the two jobs. Since the sales clerk's job pays $7.25 per hour and the attendant's job pays $7.35 per hour, the attendant's job pays more.

✓Check Your Understanding

 1. How could you have used a calculator to find the hourly rate for the gas attendant's job? Try it. How could you compare the salaries for the positions by estimating?

_____

_____

◄ Focus on the Idea

To compare two salaries, first be sure to express them in terms of the same unit of time (per hour, per day, per week, per month, or per year).

Practice

Find the weekly pay for each job.

	Job	Hours per Day	Days per Week	Hourly Rate	Weekly Pay
2.	Security guard	8	5	$7.90	_____
3.	Electician trainee	8	$5\frac{1}{2}$	$10.20	_____

Find the hourly rate for each job.

	Job	Hours per Day	Days per Week	Weekly Pay	Hourly Rate
4.	Teacher's Aid	7	5	$288.75	_____
5.	Bus driver	4	4	$120.00	_____

Extend the Idea

Suppose you wanted to find the weekly salary for the part-time sales clerk job in the newspaper ad on page 16. To find the weekly salary, use the hourly rate multiplied by the number of hours the clerk works in a week.

Step 1   Find the total number of hours worked.

$$5 \quad \text{Hours per day}$$
$$\underline{\times\,3} \quad \text{Days per week}$$
$$15 \quad \text{Hours per week}$$

Step 2   Find the total weekly salary.

$$\$7.25 \quad \text{Hourly rate}$$
$$\underline{\times\,15} \quad \text{Hours worked per week}$$
$$\$108.75 \quad \text{Total weekly salary}$$

Example: If a registered nurse earns $18.50 per hour, what is his yearly salary? Assume a 40-hour work week.

$$\$18.50$$
$$\underline{\times\,40}$$
$$\$740.00 \quad \text{Total weekly salary}$$
$$\underline{\times\,52} \quad \text{Weeks in a year}$$
$$\$38,480 \quad \text{Yearly salary}$$

✓ **Check the Math**

6. Tony's salary is $525 per week. He says he earns $26,300.00 per year. Is he correct? Explain your answer.

_____

_____

▤ **Practice**

Complete the charts. Part of the second chart is done for you.

	Hourly Rate	Hours per Week	Weekly Salary
7.	$8.75	34	_____
8.	_____	32	$300.80

	Weekly Salary	Yearly Salary	Monthly Salary
9.	$450	$23,400.00	$1,950.00
10.	_____	_____	$900.00
11.	_____	$29,100.00	_____

Apply the Idea

Read the want ads.

Help Wanted
LAWN-CARE HELPER NEEDED Part-time 16 hours a week $110.40 a week Call 555-5544. Start immediately.

Help Wanted
PART-TIME HELP NEEDED Desktop Publishing 4 hours per day 4 days per week Annual salary: $15,696 Apply in person. DataCom

Help Wanted
PART-TIME CONSTRUCTION Helper 5 days per week 5 hours per day $434.25 weekly Call High School Personnel.

Complete the chart using the want ads above.

	Job	Hourly Rate	Weekly Salary	Yearly Salary
12.	Lawn-care helper	$6.90	$110.40	$5,740.80
13.	Desktop publishing	_____	_____	_____
14.	Construction helper	_____	_____	_____

Use the information in the want ads to answer the questions.

15. How much does the lawn-care helper receive per hour?

_____

16. What is the yearly salary for the construction helper?

_____

17. How much more per hour would the construction helper earn than the lawn-care helper? _____

Write About It

18. What are some important questions to ask when you apply for a job?

_____

_____

_____

Chapter 1   Review

In This Chapter, You Have Learned
- To calculate total part-time wages
- To calculate earnings after paying job-related expenses
- To calculate total weekly earnings based on hourly rate of pay and overtime pay
- To use a time card to find the total number of hours worked
- To calculate total weekly earnings, including tips
- To calculate hourly, weekly, monthly, and yearly salaries based on information in want ads

Words You Know
Write the letter of the phrase in column 2 that best defines each word or phrase in column 1.

Column 1	Column 2
1. time card _____	a. number of hours worked beyond a regular full-time work week
2. part-time job _____	b. expenses that are necessary in order to perform a job
3. job-related expenses _____	c. amount paid for each hour of work
4. overtime _____	d. a job that requires fewer working hours than a full-time work week
5. hourly wage _____	e. a card on which the number of hours worked is recorded

More Practice
Use the chart to answer exercises 6 to 7.

Workers	Monday	Tuesday	Wednesday	Thursday	Friday
Greg	$22.75	$26.00	—	$19.50	—
Ali	$15.75	$12.50	$18.25	$16.00	—
Hannah	$30.00	$28.50	$26.75	—	—

6. After Monday, Tuesday, and Wednesday, who had earned the most, Greg, Ali, or Hannah? _____

7. How much must their employer pay Greg, Ali, and Hannah all together at the end of the week? _____

Find the amount of earnings left after paying job-related expenses.

8. Job-related expenses: $34.75 per week

   Salary: $320 per week

   Amount of earnings after paying expenses _____

Use the chart to answer exercises 9 and 10.

	Hourly Wage	Overtime Rate Over 40 Hours	Hours Worked this Week
John	$7.50	1.5	46
Helen	$13.25	2.0	44

9. What are John's total weekly earnings? _____
10. What are Helen's total weekly earnings? _____

Use the time card to find the total hours worked each day.

Time Card
Name: Matt Ortiz **Hourly Rate:** $10.50 **Job:** Restaurant Manager
Week of: 5/8 – 5/15

	DAY	DATE	TIME IN	TIME OUT	LUNCH/ DINNER	TOTAL HOURS
11.	Mon.	5/8	6:30 A.M.	4:15 P.M.	1 h	_____
12.	Wed.	5/9	3:00 P.M.	1:15 A.M.	1 h	_____

Find the total earnings.

13. If you earn $1,952.00 per month, how much do you earn per year? _____

14. If you earn $29,050 per year, how much do you earn per week? _____

Use the want ads to answer exercises 15 and 16.

Position available
INSURANCE CLERK
36 hours per week
$7.50 an hour

Wanted: Nurse's Aide
Salary: $22,950 annually

15. What is the weekly salary for the insurance clerk? _____
16. Which job pays more per year? How much more? _____
17. **For Your Portfolio** Look in the help-wanted columns of your newspaper for part-time jobs that interest you. Compare the salaries, the working hours, and any other information listed about the jobs. Create a large chart that summarizes the information you find. Use the chart and any other visual props to present your findings to the class.

Chapter 1 Practice Test

Use the chart to answer exercises 1 and 2.

Workers	Monday	Tuesday	Wednesday	Thursday	Friday
Al	$32.55	$16.75	—	$15.50	$23.55
Bob	$25.50	$35.75	$22.40	—	$19.00
Carl	$32.00	$29.40	—	$27.75	$28.65

1. How much did Al earn for the week? _____

2. What is the total that all three workers are paid at the end of the week? _____

Find the earnings after job-related expenses are paid.

3. Job-related expenses: $165.75 per month

   Salary: $1,540 per month

   Earnings after expenses: _____

Complete the chart.

		Hourly Wage	Weekly Salary	Overtime Rate	Overtime Hours	Total Earnings
4.	Anne	$6.50	$260	1.5	5	_____
5.	Marty	$5.25	$210	2.0	7	_____

Complete the time card.

Time Card
Name: Sal Ortega   **Hourly Rate:** $11.50   **Job :** Maintenance engineer
Week of: 6/15/95

	DAY	DATE	TIME IN	TIME OUT	LUNCH/ DINNER	TOTAL HOURS
6.	Mon.	6/7	6:15 A.M.	3:00 P.M.	1 h	_____
7.	Wed.	6/9	4:00 P.M.	2:00 A.M.	1 h	_____

Use the want ads at the right to answer exercises 8 to 10.

8. What is the weekly salary for the cashier?

   _____

9. If you earn $17,750 per year, how much do you earn per week? _____

10. Which job pays more per week? How much more?

    _____

Position available
CASHIER
25 hours per week
$6.25 per hour

Wanted: Data Entry Person
Salary: $17,750 annually

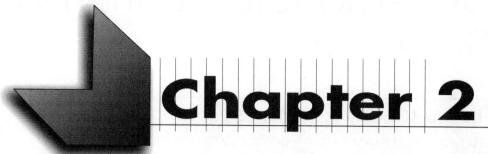

Chapter 2
Take-Home Pay

OBJECTIVES:

In this chapter, you will learn

- *To read and understand an earnings statement*
- *To calculate the total deductions subtracted from gross earnings*
- *To calculate take-home pay*
- *To use forms and tables to calculate federal income tax*
- *To complete a federal income tax return form*

This chart shows the gross pay and deductions for the year for each of three employees at a company.

YEARLY GROSS PAY	Elsa $17,654.98	Rocky $18,720.14	Max $20,360.49
Deductions for the Year:			
Federal Tax	2,740.29	1,690.72	789.45
State Tax	345.60	298.03	389.43
City Tax	88.27	——	——
FICA/Medicare Tax	1,350.53	1,432.09	1,557.58
Health Ins.	1,500.00	——	900.00
Dues	——	237.50	——

In this chapter, you will learn how to answer such questions as:

What was each employee's net pay for the year?

How much tax does each employee owe if he or she is single?

Which employees paid too much in taxes and should get a refund?

◢2•1 Understanding Earnings Statements

◢ IN THIS LESSON, YOU WILL LEARN

To read and understand an earnings statement

WORDS TO LEARN

Earnings statement *a stub attached to a paycheck that lists gross pay, deductions, and net pay*

Gross pay *the total earnings before deductions are subtracted*

Payroll deductions *the amounts subtracted from gross pay*

Taxes *the money paid to local, state, and/or federal governments*

FICA/Medicare *the money paid to government agencies for Social Security and medical insurance*

Net pay *the amount of salary that remains after all deductions have been subtracted from gross pay*

Suppose your paycheck has this earnings statement attached. What information does it give you?

EARNINGS STATEMENT		Pay period: 08/14–08/27				
Name: (Your Name Here)		Social Security #: 111-11-1111				
Gross Pay	FED TAX	STATE TAX	FICA/ MEDICARE TAX	HEALTH INS.	DUES	Net Pay
$728	$71.34	$34.35	$55.69	$30	$26.35	$510.27

New Idea

An **earnings statement** (ERN-ihngz STAYT-muhnt) lists all the information about an employee's pay and deductions. Some earnings statements list other deductions in addition to those on the statement above. **Gross pay** (grohs pay) is the total earnings before any money is deducted. **Payroll deductions** (PAY-rohl dee-DUHK-shunz) are the amounts of money withheld from your pay. Some deductions are paid to government agencies for **taxes** (TAX-uhs), to a company for health insurance, and for **FICA/Medicare** (FEYE-kuh MED-dih-kair) or social security tax, to be used for retirement. FICA/Medicare is an additional federal tax. Others are paid to a union for dues. Deductions are listed on a pay stub so the employee has a record of the money already subtracted from gross pay.

After all the deductions are subtracted from your gross pay of $728, you have $510.27 left. This is your **net pay**, (neht pay), the amount on the check you have received.

Focus on the Idea

An earnings statement shows an employee's gross pay for a given work period and any money that has been subtracted from the employee's salary for taxes or for other purposes.

Practice

Use your own words to define each of the following. The first one has been done for you.

1. Federal Tax <u>The amount of money to be paid to the U.S. government</u>

2. Gross pay _____

3. Net pay _____

Use the earnings statement on page 24 to answer exercises 4 to 6.

4. What was your deduction for state tax? _____

5. What was your deduction for FICA/Medicare tax? _____

6. What were the total deductions? _____

Apply the Idea

Some companies pay their employees every week. Others pay less often.

7. If Ray is paid twice a month, how many paychecks will he get in a year? _____

8. Katy is paid $1,185 every other Friday. Since there are 52 weeks in a year, she gets 26 paychecks. Estimate her yearly salary. _____

9. Why do you think the amount withheld for federal taxes is different for each employee?

    _____

Write About It

10. If you had a choice, how often would you want to be paid at work? Why?

    _____

    _____

◀2•2 Calculating Deductions

◀ IN THIS LESSON, YOU WILL LEARN

To calculate the total deductions subtracted from an employee's gross pay

WORDS TO LEARN

Employee benefit *a service an employer provides to its employees*

This stub shows Harry Foley's deductions from his gross pay for the past month.

FED TAX	STATE TAX	CITY TAX	FICA/ MEDICARE TAX	LIFE INS.	UNION DUES	HEALTH INS.
$153.73	$34.50	$11	$87	$24	$12.50	——

How much money was deducted from Harry's salary, or gross pay, according to the stub?

New Idea

You have learned that deductions include amounts of money subtracted from an employee's gross pay for federal, state, and local taxes. Other deductions may include insurance payments and voluntary contributions to workers' unions or to credit unions. Some employers offer an **employee benefit** (ehm-PLOY-ee BEHN-uh-fiht), such as health insurance, that they pay for the employee. (Sometimes an employer pays only part of a benefit and the employee pays the rest.) To calculate the total deductions taken from an employee's salary, add the amounts of the deductions.

Example: How much was deducted from Harry's pay?

$153.73	Federal tax
34.50	State tax
11.00	City tax
87.00	FICA/Medicare tax
24.00	Life insurance
+ 12.50	Union dues
$322.73	Total deductions

Harry had $322.73 deducted from his pay.

Focus on the Idea

To calculate the total amount of deductions from gross pay, find the sum of the deductions.

Practice

Use the chart to answer exercises 1 to 10 about the monthly deductions for five employees.

	Phil	Hector	Maria	Juanita	Kim
Federal Taxes	$134.58	$87.97	$150.00	$54.75	$157.80
State Taxes	$19.54	$11.00	$23.57	$8.50	$26.78
City Taxes	——	$2.13	——	——	$4.42
FICA/Medicare Tax	$75.00	$42.45	$82.34	$11.13	$89.56
Life Ins.	$12.00	——	$18.50	$14.00	——
Health Ins.	$34.75	$25.00	$175.09	——	——
Dues	$15.00	——	——	$23.50	$18.95

1. Who has more money deducted, Kim or Maria? _____

2. How much more? _____

3. How much money, in total, is deducted for Phil?

   _____

4. Of the five employees, who has the least amount deducted?

   _____

5. What is the amount of that deduction? _____

6. How much does Hector pay in taxes altogether?

   _____

7. Who probably receives life insurance as an employee benefit?

   _____

8. If Phil chose to stop paying for life insurance, what would be the total amount of his deductions? _____

9. Juanita's gross pay is $447.52 a week. What are her yearly earnings? _____

10. If Juanita decides to have $21.40 deducted from her pay each week for health insurance, then what will her total deductions be? _____

Write About It

11. As an employee, why is it important to know your total monthly deductions?

   _____

▶2•3 Calculating Take-Home Pay

▶**IN THIS LESSON, YOU WILL LEARN**

To calculate take-home pay

WORDS TO LEARN

Take-home pay *the net pay, or the amount of salary that remains after all deductions have been subtracted from gross pay*

This is a pay stub of an employee named Ray Suarez. How much money does Ray have left from his gross pay after deductions this month?

Gross Pay	FED TAX	STATE TAX	CITY TAX	FICA/ MEDICARE TAX	HEALTH INS	DIS. INS	DUES	Net Pay
$1,275	$128	$29	$10	$82	$158	$12.52	$21.50	?

New Idea

Take-home pay, (TAYK-hohm pay), or net pay, is the amount of salary that remains after all deductions have been subtracted from gross pay. To find take-home pay, follow these steps.

Step 1   Find the total amount of deductions. Add the deductions that appear on Ray's pay stub. Write each amount as a number of dollars and cents.

$128.00   Federal tax
   29.00   State tax
   10.00   City tax
   82.00   FICA/Medicare tax
  158.00   Health
   12.52   Disability
+ 21.50   Dues
$441.02   Total deductions

Step 2   Subtract the total deductions from the gross pay.

$1,275.00   Gross pay
− 441.02   Total deductions
$ 833.98   Ray's take-home pay for this month

Focus on the Idea

To find take-home pay, add the deductions. Then, subtract total deductions from the gross pay.

Practice

Suppose you are the payroll clerk who must make out a paycheck for an employee named Greg Wilson. Use the pay stub below to answer each question. The first one is answered for you.

Name: Greg Wilson				Social Sec.# 555-55-5555			
GROSS PAY	FED TAX	STATE TAX	CITY TAX	FICA/ MEDICARE TAX	DIS INS.	DUES PAY	NET
$1,475	$156	$39	$14	$91	—	$25.50	?

1. How can you find Greg's total deductions?
   _____*Add the deductions.*_____

2. What are Greg's total deductions? _____

3. How can you use total deductions to find Greg's take-home pay? _____

4. For what amount will you make out Greg's paycheck?
   _____

Apply the Idea

Debbie's monthly gross salary is $1,257.75. She pays $256.75 in deductions every month. Based on this, find each of the following.

5. Debbie's monthly take-home pay _____

6. Debbie's yearly gross pay _____

7. Debbie's yearly take-home pay _____

8. Debbie's total yearly deductions _____

Suzi's monthly gross pay is $1,357.87. She paid $243.50 in deductions last month. The check she received was made out for $1,601.37.

9. Was this check written for the correct amount? Explain your answer. _____

Write About It

10. Explain how the terms in each group are related.

    a. monthly deductions, monthly net pay, monthly gross pay

    _____

    b. yearly take-home pay, monthly net pay

    _____

➤2•4 Understanding Tax Forms

◀ IN THIS LESSON, YOU WILL LEARN

To use forms and tables to calculate federal income tax

WORDS TO LEARN

Income tax *the money paid to the government based on the amount of money earned*

W-2 form *a record of an employee's total payroll deductions for the year*

Tax table *a chart that lists the amount of tax that must be paid according to income and marital status*

It is early in April. This is the time of the year for you to pay your taxes. You must mail your tax return by April 15.

New Idea

Your **income tax** (IHN-kuhm taks) is the money you pay to the government. The amount is based on how much you earn. Your employer sends both you and the government a **W-2 form** (dub-uhl-yoo-TOO fawrm). It shows your earnings for the year and the taxes you have paid through payroll deductions. To complete an income tax return, you need to know three amounts.

1. Your yearly wage (appears on the W-2 form)

2. The amount of federal tax withheld, or subtracted, from your pay, for the year (appears on the W-2 form)

3. The amount of tax you owe the government

To find how much tax you owe, refer to the **tax table** (taks TAY-buhl) printed by the federal government each year. The tax table lists the amount of tax that must be paid, according to income and marital status.

Mark Stiffarm's W-2 form and a part of a tax table are shown on the next page. The W-2 form shows his gross pay for the year and the amount of money that was deducted from his salary for taxes. The tax table shows how much money a single person owes for income tax based on that person's taxable income.

a Control number		Void		
			OMB No. 1545-0008	

b Employer's identification number		1 Wages, tips, other compensation $16,765.43	2 Federal income tax withheld $2,514.81
c Employer's name, address, and ZIP code		3 Social security wages	4 Social security tax withheld $1,039.46
2-A Employer 789 Anywhere Hometown, U.S.A.		5 Medicare wages and tips	6 Medicare tax withheld $243.10
		7 Social security tips	8 Allocated tips —
d Employee's social security number		9 Advance EIC payment —	10 Dependent care benefits —
e Employees name, address, and ZIP code		11 Nonqualified plans	12 Benefits included in box 1
Mark Stiffarm 345 Anywhere Hometown, U.S.A.		13 See Instrs. for Form W-2	14 Other
		15 Stationary Deceased Pension Legal 942 Subtotal Defferred Employee plan rep. emp. compensation	

16 State Employer's state I.D. No.	17 State wages, tips, etc.	18 State income tax	19 Locality name	20 Local wages, tips, etc.	21 Local income tax

Form **W-2** Wage and Tax Statement

Department of Treasury — Internal Revenue Service
For Paperwork Reduction Act Notice, see separate instructions.

If the amount on line 37 (taxable income) is—		
At least	But less than	Tax for a single person
10,000		
10,000	10,050	1,504
10,050	10,100	1,511
10,100	10,150	1,519
10,150	10,200	1,526
10,200	10,250	1,534
10,250	10,300	1,541
10,300	10,350	1,549
10,350	10,400	1,556
10,400	10,450	1,564
10,450	10,500	1,571
10,500	10,550	1,579
10,550	10,600	1,586

Focus on the Idea

To complete your income tax return, you must use the information on your W-2 form and a tax table.

Practice

Use the W-2 form and partial tax table to answer exercises 1 to 5.

1. What was Mark Stiffarm's total yearly salary? _____

2. How much was deducted from his salary for income tax? _____

3. What does line 4 tell Mark? _____

4. If a single person's taxable income is $10,425, how much income tax will he owe? _____

5. If a single person's taxable income is $10,049, how much income tax will she owe? _____

Apply the Idea

6. Soni Yong is a single person with a taxable income of $10,368. Her employer withheld $1,429 for federal income tax. Is this too much money or not enough? By how much does it differ from the amount she owes? _____

Write About It

7. Why do you think the government charges an income tax?

_____

_____

◀2•5 Filling Out Tax Forms

▶ **IN THIS LESSON, YOU WILL LEARN**

To complete a federal income tax return form

WORDS TO LEARN

Refund *the money returned by the government if income tax deductions are too high*
Standard deduction *the amount of income that will not be taxed*

The income tax return form 1040EZ is filed by individuals who have simple tax statements. Mark Stiffarm can use this form because he is single and is planning to take only the standard deduction that the government allows for single people.

The government requires everyone with income above a given level to file a federal income tax return. If you owe tax, then you send in your payment. If the tax you paid in deductions is more than the tax you owe, then you get money back from the government. This money is called a **refund** (REE-fund).

Income Tax Return Form 1040EZ:		
Income	1. Total wages, salaries, and tips	1. ___$16,765.43___
	2. Taxable interest income of $400 or less.	2. _____
	3. Add lines 1 and 2. This is your **adjusted gross income**.	3. ___$16,765.43___
Standard Deduction	4. Can your parents claim you on their return?	
	Yes Do Worksheet on back. **No** if single, enter 6,250.	4. _____
	5. Subtract line 4 from line 3 This is your **taxable income**.	5. _____
Payments and tax	6. Enter your Federal income tax withheld from box 2 of your W-2 form(s).	6. _____
	7. **Earned income credit**	7. _____
	8. Add lines 6 and 7	8. _____
	9. **Tax.** Use the amount on line 5 to find your tax in the tax table.	9. _____
Refund or amount you owe	10. If line 8 is larger than line 9, subtract line 9 from line 8. This is your **refund**.	10. _____
	11. If line 9 is larger than line 8, subtract line 8 from line 9. This is the **amount you owe**.	11. _____

Mark Stiffarm started to fill out his Income Tax Return Form 1040EZ on page 32. Note that Line 4 on the form lists the amount of the **standard deduction** (STAN-duhrd dee-DUK-shuhn) and the personal exemption that a single person is allowed. This sum is deducted from gross income to find taxable income. For a single personlike Mark, the amount of this deduction is $6,250.

New Idea

To find how much federal tax you owe or how much your refund is, follow these steps.

Step 1   Subtract the sum of the standard deduction and personal exemption from your yearly wages to find your taxable income. The standard deduction and personal exemption for a single person is $6,250.

Step 2   To find Mark's taxable income, subtract:

$16,765.43   Yearly wages
−6,250.00   Standard deduction/personal exemption
$10,515.43   Taxable income

Step 3   Now, look back at the federal tax table to find the tax owed on Mark's taxable income. The table shows that the tax Mark owes is $1,579.

Step 4   Subtract the tax owed on his taxable income from the amount of federal tax he had withheld for the year.

$2,514.81   Federal tax withheld
−1,579.00   Tax owed
$ 935.81   Refund

Last year, Mark had more money withheld than he owed. So, instead of paying more taxes, he will get a refund.

✓Check the Math

1. José says his yearly wages were $50 more than Mark's, so he earned $16,815.43. Yet he says his taxes are the same as Mark's. Is he right? How can you tell?

◀ **Focus on the Idea**

When you complete an income tax return, you find out either how much tax you owe or how much of a refund you get.

Practice

Use the information at the beginning of this lesson and the W-2 form and tax table on page 31 to answer exercises 2 to 6. The first one is done for you.

2. Where did Mark find the information he needed to complete Line 9 on Form 1040EZ? ___tax table___

3. Where did he find how much in federal taxes were withheld for the year? _____

4. What amount should he write on line 4 on Form 1040EZ? _____

5. What line tells him if he gets a refund? _____

6. What line tells him how much he still owes in income tax? _____

Extend the Idea

Sometimes an employer does not withhold enough money from an employee's paycheck to pay the amount of federal income tax owed. Suppose Mark's W-2 form showed that, instead of having $2,514.81 withheld, only $1,533 was withheld. How would this change his income tax return? To find how much money he would owe, subtract the amount withheld from the tax owed.

$1,579	Tax owed
−1,533	Tax withheld
$ 46	Tax still owed

Not enough money was withheld. Mark would owe $46 more in taxes.

✓Check Your Understanding

7. Suppose you know the total tax owed on your income and how much tax was withheld. Without calculating, how can you find out whether you will receive a refund from the government, or whether you still owe money?

_____

Practice

Use the tax table on page 31 and the W-2 form on page 35 to answer exercises 8 to 10.

8. How much money was deducted from Olga's pay for taxes?

   _____

9. How much is Olga's taxable income after she subtracts the standard deduction and her personal exemption?

   _____

a Control number		Void		INFORMATION RETURN For State, City or Employer File Copy D	
			OMB No. 1545-0008		
b Employer's identification number				1 Wages, tips, other compensation $16,279.54	2 Federal income tax withheld $2,129.87
c Employer's name, address, and ZIP code 2-A Employer 789 Anywhere Hometown, U.S.A.				3 Social security wages	4 Social security tax withheld $1,513.13
				5 Medicare wages and tips	6 Medicare tax withheld
				7 Social security tips	8 Allocated tips
d Employee's social security number				9 Advance EIC payment	10 Dependent care benefits
e Employees name, address, and ZIP code Olga Blume 234 Anywhere Hometown, U.S.A.				11 Nonqualified plans	12 Benefits included in box 1
				13 See Instrs. for Form W-2	14 Other
				15 Statutory Deceased Pension Legal 942 Subtotal Deferred Employee plan rep. emp. compensation	
16 State Employer's state I.D. No.	17 State wages, tips, etc.	18 State income tax	19 Locality name	20 Local wages, tips, etc.	21 Local income tax

Department of Treasury — Internal Revenue Service

Form **W-2** Wage and Tax Statement

For Paperwork Reduction Act Notice, see separate instructions.

10. Will Olga get a refund or will she owe taxes? Explain.

_____

_____

Apply the Idea

11. Would a single person with a taxable income of $12,849 pay more income tax than Mark? _____

12. If a single person had a taxable income of $13,400 and paid $2,396.00 in federal tax, do you think he or she will get a refund? Explain your answer.

_____

_____

Write About It

13. How do a standard deduction and a personal exemption affect the amount of tax a worker will pay?

_____

_____

_____

Chapter 2   Review

In This Chapter, You Have Learned
- To read and understand an earnings statement
- To calculate the total amount of deductions subtracted from gross earnings
- To calculate take-home pay
- To use forms and tables to calculate federal income tax
- To complete a federal income tax return

Words You Know

From the lists of "Words to Learn," choose the word or phrase that best completes each statement.

1. An amount subtracted from your earnings is called a(n) _____ .

2. _____ is the amount of your salary you receive after paying all deductions.

3. Money taken from your salary for the local, state or federal government is a(n) _____ .

4. Services that a company offers its employees are called _____ .

5. _____ is a record of yearly earnings and deductions.

6. The amount of income that is not taxed is a(n) _____ .

More Practice

Refer to the earnings statement on page 23 to answer exercises 7 to 9.

7. What cost Elsa $88.27? _____

8. How much did Max have left after he paid his deductions? _____

9. How much did Rocky pay for federal taxes? _____

Use the income tax return on page 32 to answer exercises 10 to 12.

10. What information should be written on line 1? _____

11. On which line could you find yearly gross salary? _____

12. What is the source of the amount $16,765.43? _____

Problems You Can Solve

13. Jaime's gross pay is $1,600 per month. He pays $274.50 in deductions each month. What is his yearly take-home pay?

_____

14. Barbara Freeman has payroll deductions of $57.80 for federal taxes, $21.50 for state taxes, and $42.75 for FICA/Medicare taxes. What are her total deductions?

_____

15. Ann's gross pay for the month is $1,100. She had $105.75 deducted for federal taxes, $32 for state taxes, $75.89 for FICA/Medicare taxes and $13.50 for union dues. What were Ann's total deductions? _____

16. According to exercise 15 above, what was Ann's take-home pay? _____

17. Use the following information and the tax table on page 31 to determine whether or not Mary, whose salary information follows, is entitled to get a refund. _____

Gross yearly salary	$16,789
Federal tax withheld	$ 1,489
Taxable income	$10,539

18. Lorenzo's gross monthly pay was $1,245.63. His deductions were $35.14, $89.21, $23.40, and $14.50. Find his net pay.

_____

19. **For Your Portfolio** Look in the newspaper for some want ads for employment. Use the chart below to show what each job would pay for a yearly salary. See if you can find out your state and city tax rates. How much take-home pay would each job you found actually pay?

Job	SALARY Monthly/ Weekly	Yearly	TAXES Federal	State	City	TAKE-HOME PAY

Chapter 2   Practice Test

Use the earnings statement to answer exercises 1 to 5.

Monthly Earnings Statement:					Pay Period: 2/1–2/28			
Employee: Joan Smith					Soc. Sec. # 222-22-2220			
Gross Pay	Taxes				Insurance			Net Pay
	Fed	State	City	FICA/Medicare	Health	Dis.	Dues	
$909	$81	$14	$2.16	$60	$111	—	—	$640.24

1. How much was deducted from Joan's pay for health insurance? _____

2. Why was $60 deducted? _____

3. How much was deducted for taxes? _____

4. Why was $14 deducted? _____

5. Were more taxes withheld for the federal, state, or city government? _____

Use this list of deductions for three employees to answer exercises 6 to 10.

	Leroy	David	Casey
Federal Taxes	$157.98	$53.25	$102.00
State Taxes	43.00	12.50	35.75
City Taxes	10.54	1.75	—
FICA/Medicare tax	102.00	39.70	75.65
Life Ins.	24.50	—	19.95
Health Ins.	100.00	—	—
Dues	—	$ 5.25	$ 18.75

6. Who did not have a deduction for life insurance? _____

7. What was the total of David's deductions? _____

8. What was the total Leroy paid in taxes? _____

9. Whose total deductions were greater, Leroy's or Casey's? How much greater?

_____

10. If Casey had not paid for life insurance, how would his total deductions have changed?

_____

_____

Chapter 3
Budgeting

OBJECTIVES:

In this chapter, you will learn

- *To estimate and calculate average monthly expenses*
- *To find average fixed and variable expenses*
- *To display and interpret budget information in a chart*
- *To use a budget based on income*
- *To adjust a budget to pay for unexpected expenses*

Lou wants to move out of his parents' home and rent his own apartment. He has found three apartments he likes, but is not sure if he can afford them.

	Apartment 1	Apartment 2	Apartment 3
Rent	$675	$875	$520
Electric	45	(landlord pays)	38
Gas	97	(landlord pays)	68

Lou's Monthly Budget	
Income: $1,127	
Fixed Expenses	
Rent	_____
Electric	_____
Gas	_____
Variable Expenses	
Food	$ 145
Entertainment	125
Savings	40
Total Expenses	_____

By the end of this chapter, you will have learned how to balance a budget so that you can help Lou choose the best apartment that he can afford on his budget.

3•1 Finding Average Monthly Expenses

IN THIS LESSON, YOU WILL LEARN

To estimate and calculate average monthly expenses

WORDS TO LEARN

Expense *the cost for something you bought, rented, or otherwise paid for*

Average *the typical value of a group of numbers*

Kevin made a chart to record his expenses.

	Kevin's Expenses		
Items	**January**	**February**	**March**
Rent	$625.00	$625.00	$625.00
Electric	32.70	34.75	29.80
Life insurance	8.95	8.95	8.95
Groceries	147.26	112.93	134.52
Car loan	209.75	209.75	209.75
Telephone	56.20	63.14	68.42

How can you use a calculator to find Kevin's average monthly expenses? How can you check to be sure your answer is reasonable?

New Idea

An **expense** (ehk-SPENS) is the cost of an item you buy, rent, or otherwise pay for. When trying to meet a budget, it is important to be able to find your average expenses. To find an **average** (AV-uhr-ihj), add the amounts for a group of items. Then divide the total by the number of items. It is always a good idea to estimate the average before calculating, by rounding the amounts to a convenient number.

⤷Remember

One method of estimating is to round each amount so that there is one non-zero digit. So, 625 rounds to 600, 8.95 rounds to 10, and 56.20 rounds to 60. If the digit to the right of the rounding place is 5 or more, round up. If the digit to the right of the rounding place is less than 5, round down.

$$625 \rightarrow 600 \qquad 8.95 \rightarrow 10 \qquad 56.20 \rightarrow 60$$

less than 5   greater than 5   greater than 5

To find Kevin's average monthly expenses:

Step 1   Estimate.

Kevin rounded his monthly expenses for January. Then he added the rounded amounts mentally:

$600 + $30 + $10 + $100 + $200 + $60 = $1,000

Since his February and March expenses were similar, Kevin used the $1,000 estimate for each of the three months.

Step 2   Compute the actual amount.

Add each set of monthly expenses. Then find the total for all three months. Kevin used a calculator.

January: $625 + $32.70 + $8.95 + $147.26 + $209.75 + $56.20 = $1,079.86

February: $625 + $34.75 + $8.95 + $112.93 + $209.75 + $63.14 = $1,054.52

March: $625 + $29.80 + $8.95 + $134.52 + $209.75 + $68.42 = $1,076.44

The total for the three months is:

$1,079.86 + $1,054.52 + $1,076.44 = $3,210.82

Kevin divided his three-month total by the number of months to find the average monthly expenses.

$3,210.82 ÷ 3 = $1,070.27

Kevin's estimate of $1,000 is close to his calculated answer of $1,070.27, so he knows his answer is reasonable.

Kevin could have used his calculator another way to find his three-month total. He could have input the monthly expenses for all three months without pressing the 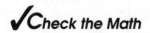 key until after he input the last amount. Try this and see if your total matches Kevin's.

✓Check the Math

1. Matt's total expenses for each of three months were $423, $578, and $495. He calculated his average monthly expenses to be $371.67. Use estimation to check if his answer is reasonable. Explain how you estimated the amount.

_____

_____

_____

Focus on the Idea

To find a monthly average of expenses, first estimate. Then add the expenses for several months and divide the total amount by the number of months. Use your estimate to check whether your calculated answer makes sense.

Practice

Answer each question. The first one is done for you.

2. Explain how to estimate the average of the following amounts:
   $625, $135, $290

   Round: $625 to $600, $135 to $100, and $290 to $300

   Add: $600 + $100 + $300 = $1,000

   Divide: $1,000 ÷ 3 = $333.33

   Round to the nearest ten's place: $333.33 to $330

3. Explain how to find the actual average for the amounts in exercise 2.

   _____

   _____

   _____

   _____

The chart shows total monthly expenses for three people. Complete the chart by first estimating each person's average monthly expenses. Then find the actual averages.

			TOTAL EXPENSES			
					Monthly Average	
	April	May	June	July	Estimated	Calculated
4. Gino	$1,876	$250	$2,329	$1,098	_____	_____
5. Marco	876	98	478	12	_____	_____
6. Vera	721	42	390	587	_____	_____

Use the following list of expenses for exercises 7 to 9.

Jamie's Expenses			
Items	January	February	March
Rent	$800.00	$800.00	$800.00
Electric	37.40	40.00	39.50
Health insurance	175.00	175.00	175.00
Groceries	110.00	102.00	100.00
Heat	87.00	87.00	87.00
Telephone	35.00	27.00	32.00

7. Estimate Jamie's average monthly expenses. _____

8. Use a calculator or pencil and paper to find Jamie's actual average monthly expenses. _____

9. How does your estimate help you decide if your calculated answer is correct?

_____

Apply the Idea

10. Hal pays $750 every month for rent and $120 a month during the winter for gas. His electric bills for December, January, and February were $57.54, $34.89, and $47. His phone bills were $45, $38, and $42.35. Hal paid $125 in groceries for January and February, and $150 for groceries for December. Use this information to complete the chart.

Hal's Expenses			
Items	December	January	February
Rent	_____	_____	_____
Gas	_____	_____	_____
Electric	_____	_____	_____
Phone	_____	_____	_____
Groceries	_____	_____	_____

a. Estimate Hal's average monthly expenses. _____

b. Calculate Hal's average monthly expenses. _____

Write About It

11. List your monthly expenses. Estimate the cost of each. Then find an estimated total.

_____

_____

_____

3•2 Average Fixed and Variable Expenses

IN THIS LESSON, YOU WILL LEARN

To estimate and calculate fixed and variable monthly expenses

WORDS TO LEARN

Fixed expenses *expenses that remain the same over a period of time*

Board *the expenses for meals*

Variable expenses *expenses that may change from one time period to the next*

Marielle has a part-time job and lives at home. The chart shows all her expenses for the month of February. What is the average of Marielle's weekly fixed expenses? What is the average of Marielle's weekly variable expenses?

Marielle's Weekly Expenses				
	Week 1	Week 2	Week 3	Week 4
Room and Board	$40.00	$ 40.00	$40.00	$40.00
Entertainment	10.75	12.90	25.00	5.50
Gasoline	10.89	9.49	12.60	6.83
Clothing	45.92	0	15.04	18.47
School supplies	4.50	32.65	7.50	2.98
Telephone	5.80	5.80	5.80	5.80
Car insurance	125.00	0	0	0

New Idea

To find the average of **fixed expenses** (fihkst ehk-SPENS-uhz), identify which expenses stay the same from one period of time to the next. For Marielle, monthly fixed expenses include room, the expenses for meals, or **board** (bawrd), telephone, and car insurance, which she pays in the first week of each month.

Find Marielle's average weekly fixed expenses. Estimate first. Add to find the total amount of fixed expenses for each week. Find the sum of the weekly totals and divide it by the number of weeks.

$170.80 + $45.80 + $45.80 + $45.80 (total expenses for 4 weeks) = $308.20
    Divide: $308.20 ÷ 4 = $77.05 average weekly fixed expenses

Variable expenses (VAIR-ee-uh-buhl ehk-SPENS-uhz) are expenses that do not stay the same from one period to the next. Marielle's variable expenses are entertainment, gasoline, clothing, and school supplies.

To find the average variable expenses, follow the same method you used to find the average fixed expenses.

Focus on the Idea

To find average fixed or variable expenses, add all the fixed or variable expenses; then divide the total by the number of units of time.

Practice

Use the chart for exercises 1 to 6.

	Monthly Expenses		
Items	Month 1	Month 2	Month 3
Rent	$525.00	$525.00	$525.00
Telephone	42.50	35.00	59.76
Electric	43.72	47.29	39.45
Gas	106.14	78.51	41.39
Food	150.08	125.37	200.95
Life insurance	12.50	12.50	12.50

1. Which expenses are fixed?

   _____

2. Which expenses are variable?

   _____

3. Estimate the average monthly fixed expenses.

   _____

4. Calculate the average of the monthly fixed expenses.

   _____

5. Estimate the average monthly variable expenses.

   _____

6. Calculate the average of the monthly variable expenses.

   _____

Apply the Idea

7. Jean's fixed expenses for four weeks in February totaled $350. The total of her variable expenses was $212.50.

   a. What was the average of Jean's weekly fixed expenses?

   _____

   b. What was the average of Jean's weekly variable expenses? _____

Write About It

8. Choose two of your own variable expenses. Suggest some ways you can lower these expenses.

   _____

   _____

▶3•3 Making a Monthly Budget

IN THIS LESSON, YOU WILL LEARN
To display and interpret budget information in a chart

WORDS TO LEARN
Leisure activities *activities done for fun*
Budget *a plan for how to spend money*

Bill pays $535 per month in rent. He also spends an average of $12.50 per week for gasoline, $40 per week for groceries, $59 per month for electricity, $23.50 per month for telephone, and $25 per week for **leisure activities** (LEE-zhur ak-TIHV-uh-teez) such as movies and sporting events. Bill wants to save at least $15 per week. What will his monthly **budget** (BUHJ-iht), or his plan for spending money, look like?

New Idea

You can find Bill's monthly budget by changing his weekly expenses to monthly expenses. To do this, multiply each weekly expense by 52 (weeks in a year). Then, divide by 12 (months in a year). Or, multiply the weekly expenses by 4.3, which is equal to 52 ÷ 12.

Item	Average Monthly Cost
Rent	$ 535.00
Electric	59.00
Telephone	23.50
Gasoline	53.75
Groceries	172.00
Leisure	107.50
Savings	+ 64.50
Total	$1,015.25

Gasoline: $12.50 per week × 4.3 = $53.75 per month
Groceries: $40 per week × 4.3 = $172.00 per month
Leisure: $25 per week × 4.3 = $107.50 per month
Savings: $15 per week × 4.3 = $64.50 per month

Bill's monthly budget is shown in this chart.

Focus on the Idea
To make a budget, find the total monthly expenses for each item. Then list the expenses in a chart.

✓Check Your Understanding

1. Bill needed to reduce his expenses to spend less than $1,000 a month because of a pay cut. He decided to spend $13 a week less on leisure activities. Would this reduce his monthly expenses enough? Explain.

_____

_____

Practice

Answer each question. The first one is done for you.

2. Suppose you have a job and pay $15 per week to your parents for board.

   a. Would you list this board as a fixed expense or as a variable expense in a budget? _Fixed expense_

   b. How much would you list under "board" in a monthly budget? Explain your answer.

   _____

3. Suppose you want to put aside $20 per week for savings.

   a. If you were serious about saving the money, where would you list this expense in a budget? _____

   b. How much would you list under "savings" in a monthly budget? _____

Find the monthly expense for each of the following.

4. $7 per week for school supplies and books _____

5. $125 per week for rent _____

6. $234 per year for life insurance payments _____

Use the following budget to answer exercises 7 to 10.

7. What is the total of Beth's fixed expenses for the month? _____

8. What is the total of Beth's variable expenses for the month? _____

9. How much does Beth plan to save each week? _____

10. How much does Beth plan to spend on entertainment in a year? _____

Beth's Monthly Budget	
Fixed Expenses	**Amount per Month**
Mortgage	$1,160.00
Car lease	229.00
Variable Expenses	
Gas	102.13
Telephone	35.80
Savings	40.00
Electric	58.50
Food	250.75
Entertainment	+100.00
Total Expenses	$1,976.18

✏ Write About It

11. Suppose you had expenses for the following: *school supplies, carfare, leisure activities, clothing, food,* and *savings*. Decide on an amount of money for each. Then make a monthly budget that shows these expenses. Label your expenses as fixed or variable, and explain why you labeled them the way you did.

   _____

   _____

   _____

►3•4 Using a Budget

► IN THIS LESSON, YOU WILL LEARN

To use a budget based on income

WORDS TO LEARN

Balanced budget *a budget based on an income that is at least as much as the expenses*

Debt *money owed that must be repaid, or an amount spent beyond the income*

Jack's take-home pay is $1,240 a month. He began the budget in the chart.

Jack didn't finish his budget because the amount he spends on food and entertainment can be changed depending on the amount of money he has available. What might Jack's food and entertainment expenses be so that he will have a balanced budget?

Monthly Budget	
Fixed Expenses	**Amount**
Rent	$ 525
Car lease	169
Variable Expenses	
Telephone	25
Electric	32
Food	_____
Entertainment	_____
Total Expenses	$ _____

New Idea

A **balanced budget** (BAL-uhnst BUHJ-iht) is a budget based on spending an amount of money that is less than or equal to what you earn. To find out how much Jack can spend on food and entertainment, follow these steps:

Step 1   Find the total of the expenses listed:

$525 + $169 + $25 + $32 = $751

Step 2   Subtract this total from Jack's income:

$1,240 − $751 = $489

Step 3   The total expenses should not be more than the amount of income. Choose a realistic amount for one expense; then subtract to find out how much is left for the other.

$489   total amount Jack has available
−200   amount for food
$289   amount for entertainment

If Jack spends more than his take-home pay, he will have to borrow money to meet expenses. This borrowed money will be a **debt** (deht), money that he must repay at some time.

Focus on the Idea

To balance a budget, plan variable expenses so that fixed expenses and variable expenses are less than or equal to income.

Practice

Compare the income and total expenses. Write *yes* or *no* to tell whether the budget is balanced. The first one is done for you.

	Income	Total Expenses	Balanced
1.	$1,245	$1,145	yes
2.	985	1,076	_____
3.	1,487	1,487	_____

Complete the chart by finding the amount of savings. The total of the fixed and variable expenses plus savings should equal the income. All items are monthly amounts.

	Income	Fixed Expenses	Variable Expenses	Savings
4.	$2,345	$1,100	$500	_____
5.	650	220	159	_____
6.	1,234	456	77	_____

Apply the Idea

7. Greg's net pay is $1,890 per month. His rent is $675 per month, and he makes a monthly car payment of $189. His average monthly telephone bill is $36, and his electric bill is always $56. Greg would like to plan his savings and entertainment expenses. Write a budget that Greg can use based on this income and these expenses.

Greg's Budget	
_____	_____
_____	_____
_____	_____
_____	_____
_____	_____
_____	_____

Write About It

8. Briefly explain how a balanced budget differs from an unbalanced budget. Be sure to include how income and expenses are related in both budgets.

_____

_____

_____

►3•5 Adjusting a Budget

►IN THIS LESSON, YOU WILL LEARN

To adjust a budget to pay for unexpected expenses

WORDS TO LEARN

Adjust *fix or change by reducing or increasing*

Sandy's Monthly Budget	
Income: $ 874	
Fixed Expenses	
Room and board	$ 300
Car loan	159
Variable Expenses	
Telephone	$ 25
Food	80
Entertainment	160
Gas and car repair	100
Savings	50
Total Expenses	$ 874

Sandy has been looking for a new computer. One store is selling the computer she wants for $1,300. The dealer said she could purchase it by paying $110 a month for 12 months. How can Sandy adjust her budget so that she can afford this new expense?

New Idea

To **adjust** (uh-JUST) or change a budget, subtract from or add to variable expenses. Always keep the total expenses less than or equal to the income.

Sandy must subtract $110 from her variable expenses so her total expenses are still less than or equal to her income.

Step 1 Decide which variable expenses to reduce. Possible choices for Sandy are entertainment, savings, and food.

Step 2 Estimate how much can be subtracted from each to add up to Sandy's new expense. Make adjustments.

Step 3 Determine how much more is needed.

Step 4 Rewrite Sandy's old budget by making the adjustments to create a new budget.

New Budget for Sandy			
Items	Old Budget	Adjustment	New Budget
Income: $874			
Fixed Expenses			
Room and board	$300		$300
Car loan	159		159
Variable Expenses			
Telephone	$ 25		$ 25
Food	80	−$20	60
Entertainment	160	− $50	110
Gas and car repair	100		100
Savings	50	−$40	10
Computer payments	0	+ $110	110
Total Expenses	$874		$874

Focus on the Idea

A budget can be adjusted to reflect changing or unexpected expenses.

Practice

Use Sandy's budget to answer the following questions.

1. Suppose Sandy had used only $20 from entertainment and then used $30 from gas and car repair. What would these two expenses have been in her adjusted budget?

   _____

2. Could Sandy afford a computer that cost $150 a month if she used an additional $30 from "gas and car repair" in her old budget for her new budget? Why or why not?

   _____

Use the chart to answer exercises 3 to 6.

3. What are Keith's total expenses? _____
4. Is this budget balanced? How can you tell?

   _____

5. Keith wants to take a weekly guitar lesson. Each lesson will cost $15. How much per month will the lessons cost? _____

6. Which expenses can Keith adjust so that he can include the guitar lessons in his budget and still keep his total expenses the same?

   _____

Keith's Monthly Budget	
Item	Amount
Income: $1,075	
Fixed Expenses	
Rent	$450
Loan payment	120
Variable Expenses	
Telephone	$ 45
Electric	50
Groceries	140
Leisure activities	175
Savings	95
Total Expenses	_____

Apply the Idea

7. Nick has a part-time job. His monthly income is $375.75. From this income, he must pay $42 a month for carfare to school; $7.50 a week for school lunch; $30.00 a week for a math tutor, and $35 a month for cable TV. He spends an average of $25 each weekend going out with his friends. In the margin, make a monthly budget for Nick, showing how much he could save each month.

Write About It

8. Explain why you cannot use money from fixed expenses in order to adjust a budget.

   _____

Chapter 3   Review

In This Chapter, You Have Learned
- To estimate and calculate average monthly expenses
- To find average fixed and variable expenses
- To display, interpret, use, and adjust budget information in a chart

Words You Know

From the lists of "Words to Learn," choose the word or phrase that best completes each statement.

1. Expenses that remain the same every month are _____.

2. A(n) _____ is an amount of money owed that must be repaid for expenses beyond your income.

3. A(n) _____ is a plan that shows how you spend your money.

4. If your income is greater than or equal to your expenses, the budget is _____.

5. _____ your budget to reflect increases in your expenses.

More Practice

The chart shows total monthly expenses for two people. Complete the chart by estimating first, and then find each person's monthly expenses.

	March	April	May	June	Total Expenses Estimated	Total Expenses Calculated	Monthly Average
6.	$426	$288	$178	$99	_____	_____	_____
7.	521	420	398	87	_____	_____	_____

Problems You Can Solve

Use the chart to answer exercises 8 to 10.

8. Which expenses are fixed?

   _____

9. What are the average monthly fixed expenses?

   _____

10. What are the average monthly changing expenses?

   _____

Items	Monthly Expenses Month 1	Month 2	Month 3
Rent	$500.00	$500.00	$500.00
Telephone	32.50	29.00	39.75
Electric	33.00	40.00	30.00
Food	100.00	95.00	120.00
Life insurance	15.50	15.50	15.50

11. José earns $1,500 a month from his job. He pays $625 a month in rent. He also spends an average of $20 a week for gasoline, $40 a week on groceries, $48 a month for electricity, and $20 a week for leisure activities such as movies and sporting events. José wants to save at least $10 a week towards a new compact disc player. Complete José's monthly budget.

José's Monthly Budget	
Income: $_____	
Fixed Expenses	
_____	_____
Variable Expenses	
_____	_____
_____	_____
_____	_____
_____	_____
Total Expenses	_____

Complete Joe's budget so that it is balanced.

Joe's Monthly Budget	
Income: $335	
Fixed Expenses	
School lunch	50
Carfare	110
Variable Expenses	
12. Entertainment	_____
13. Clothes	_____
14. Savings	_____
15. **Total Expenses**	_____

Use the following budget to complete exercises 16 and 17.

16. Maryann will receive a raise in salary next month. However, her rent will also be increased to $475 per month. How much of a raise must she receive in order to keep her present budget balanced?

_____

Maryann's Monthly Budget	
Income: $878	
Fixed Expense	
Rent	425
Variable Expenses	
Telephone	34
Entertainment	150
Clothing	225
Savings	44
Total Expenses	$878

17. Adjust this budget (with the rent at $475 and the appropriate pay raise) so that it remains in balance but allows Maryann to afford car-loan payments of $150 per month.

18. **For Your Portfolio**   Work with a partner to complete the problem on page 39. Help Lou adjust his budget so he can rent an apartment. Then adjust his budget so that Lou can also afford to have cable TV installed at a cost of $50 per month. Discuss which expenses you will transfer from his old budget to his new budget and how much you will need to transfer from each. Rewrite his new budget in the margin.

1. Janet's expenses were as follows: January–$675; February–$785; March–$639; April–$590.

   a. Estimate her average monthly expenses. _____

   b. Calculate her average monthly expenses. _____

   c. Suppose in May her expenses were twice as much as in April. Now what are her average monthly expenses?

   _____

Use the list of expenses for exercises 2 to 4.

2. Which expenses are fixed?

   _____

3. What are the average monthly fixed expenses?

   _____

4. What are the average monthly variable expenses?

   _____

Items	Month 1	Month 2	Month 3
Rent	$580	$580	$580
Telephone	35	35	56
Food	125	110	115
Car insurance	150	150	150

Use the following budget for exercises 5 to 10.

5. Why is Bart's loan payment listed under fixed expenses?

   _____

6. What are Bart's total monthly expenses?

   _____

7. Suppose Bart spent only $100 per month on leisure activities. How much could he save and still have a balanced budget?

   _____

8. Suppose Bart did not have a telephone. How much more could he spend on leisure activities and food and still have a balanced budget?

   _____

Bart's Monthly Budget	
Income: $1,245	
Fixed Expenses	
Rent	$675
Loan Payment	130
Variable Expenses	
Telephone	34
Food	275
Leisure Activities	121
Savings	10
Total Expenses	___

9. Bart has just put cable TV in his house. This means an additional expense of $45 per month. Use the margin to rewrite and adjust Bart's budget so that it is still balanced.

10. Bart's salary will be raised to $1,350 per month starting next month. Adjust his budget again to include cable TV payments of $45 per month. Be sure the budget remains in balance.

Chapter 4
Personal Banking

OBJECTIVES:

In this chapter, you will learn

- *To write checks and balance a checking account*
- *To compare and adjust a personal check register to agree with a monthly bank statement*
- *To understand how to use a passbook for a savings account*
- *To calculate simple interest on a loan balance*
- *To calculate interest compounded annually, quarterly, and monthly*
- *To calculate fixed and variable interest rates on loans*
- *To calculate and compare the costs of monthly loan payments*

Personal Savings and Loan

Savings Account Interest Rates:
3% annual rate,
compounded quarterly

Certificates of Deposit (CD):
5% annual rate for 1 year
6.5% annually for 3 years

Checking Account Fees:
$4.50 per month service fee
No fee per check

Personal Loans:
12.5% annual rate for up to 5 years

Keith and Kelly use the Personal Savings and Loan as their bank. Keith has some money he wants to start saving for a new car. He needs to know how much interest the bank will pay him if he puts his money into a savings account or a CD. Kelly wants to borrow some money so she can buy a new computer. She needs to know how much she will have to pay the bank in interest if she borrows money. You can find some of the answers to their questions by reading the information on the bank sign above.

Managing a Checking Account

To write checks and balance a checking account

WORDS TO LEARN

Deposit *to put money into a checking account or savings account*

Check register *a personal record of checking account activity*

Account balance *amount available in an account*

Withdrawal *amount taken out of an account*

Transaction *any activity in an account that changes the balance*

Greg wants to join a health club but must first pay his auto insurance. To decide if he can afford both, he looks at the balance in his checkbook. Will he have enough money in his account for both payments?

New Idea

It is important to keep your own record of the activity in your checking account. To make a **deposit** (dih-PAW-ziht), or put money into an account, you use a deposit slip. You write your name, the date, and list the amount of any cash and checks that you are depositing.

A personal record of your checking account activity is written in a **check register** (chehk REH-jihs-ter). It is important to keep track of your **account balance** (uh-KOWNT BA-luhns), the amount of money available in your account, in your check register. A **withdrawal** (wihth-DRAW-uhl) is the amount of money taken out of an account. Any activity that changes the balance is a **transaction** (trans-AK-shuhn). After making his deposits and payments, will Greg be able to join the health club if he needs $125 for the first payment?

Greg has $45.75 in his account. He has $25 in cash and a check for $92.50 to deposit. He must pay his insurance bill of $95.50. This is his deposit slip.

Bank ABC

Deposit Slip

Name: *Greg Johnson*

Account no. *110-111-111*

Date *May 5, 199—*

	Dollars/Cents	
Cash	$ 25	00
Checks	$ 92	50
Total from other side	00	00
TOTAL	$ 117	50

To write a check for his insurance, Greg writes the date and the name of the company that will receive the check. He writes the amount first as a number, then in words. Finally, he signs his name.

```
┌─────────────────────────────────────────────────────────────────────┐
│  Greg Johnson                                               201       │
│  182 Prince Street              May 6  19 9-    00-00/000             │
│  Anytown, U.S.A.                                                      │
│                                                                       │
│  PAY TO THE                                                           │
│  ORDER OF   Fender Auto Insurance              $  95.50              │
│                                                                       │
│   Ninety-five and  50/100 ────────────────────────────── DOLLARS     │
│  Bank ABC                                                             │
│                                                                       │
│  MEMO     Auto Insurance               Greg Johnson                  │
└─────────────────────────────────────────────────────────────────────┘
```

Greg's own record of his account balance must match the bank's balance. To do this, he must do the following:

Step 1 Add the amount of any deposits to the balance.

$ 45.75 balance
+ 117.50 deposits
$163.25 new balance

Step 2 Subtract the amounts of any checks written, but not yet cashed, from the new balance.

$163.25 new balance
− 95.50 check written
$ 67.75 final balance

Step 3 Greg's check register records all deposits and checks.

DATE	CHECK NUMBER	ISSUED TO	DEPOSIT	WITHDRAWAL	BALANCE
5/4					$ 45.75
5/5			$117.50		$ 163.25
5/6	201	Fender Auto Insurance		$ 95.50	$ 67.75

Greg's balance is not enough for the $125 club membership.

✓Check Your Understanding

1. Would it have made a difference if Greg had written his check first, and then made the deposit? Why or why not?

◄ Focus on the Idea

To balance a checking account, add the amounts of the deposits and subtract the amounts of the checks written. The balance should be greater than the total amount of the checks written.

Practice

Use the information in Greg's check register to answer exercises 2 to 5.

2. How did Greg determine that $117.50 was his deposit?

_____

3. On May 7, Greg wrote checks for $26.70 and $32.50. What is his new balance? _____

4. On May 9, Greg deposited a check he received from his grandmother for $43.50 and another he received from his uncle for $25.00. What is his new balance? _____

Extend the Idea

To complete the balancing of his checking account, Greg must subtract the amounts of fees charged by his bank. These include:
- A fee for each check written
- A monthly service charge
- A fee for printing new checks

Example: Compare the cost of fees in the following banks.

Fee Schedules

Bank	Fee per Check	Monthly Service Charge	Check Printing
Farmers Bank	none	$4.50 (none if balance remains above $1,000)	$8.50 per 200 checks
Soldiers Bank	$0.10	$2.50	$7.50 per 200 checks
Teachers Bank	No fee for first 10 checks per month; then $0.12 per check	none	$8.00 per 200 checks

✓Check the Math

5. Jamie has a checking account at the Farmers Bank. In July, he had a balance of $500 and wrote 15 checks. He said the bank would not charge him a service charge for the month. Is he correct? Explain your answer.

_____

Practice

Suppose you have a balance of $975. You write 32 checks in one month and have 200 new checks printed. What fee will each bank charge you? The first one has been done for you.

6. Farmers Bank $13.00   7. Soldiers Bank _____   8. Teachers Bank _____

Suppose you have a checking account balance of $437.50. Find the new balance after each transaction.

	Transaction number	Deposit	Withdrawal	Balance
				$437.50
9.	1	$35.85	—	_____
10.	2	—	$256.85	_____
11.	3	$100	$250	_____

12. Suppose your bank has a monthly service charge of $5.50, and it charges $.25 per check. Starting with your balance in exercise 11, subtract the bank's charges for two checks and the monthly fee. What is your new balance? _____

Apply the Idea

The High-Tech Bank charges a $4.50 per month service charge and has no per check fee. Complete the check register for the following transactions in an account with a balance of $376.80.

March 5: Check 560, written to Natural Gas Co. for $51.78

March 8: A deposit of $124.75 in cash and checks

March 12: Check 561 written to Berger's Store for $150.54

March 21: Check 562 written to Right Way Supermarket for $75

	DATE	CHECK NUMBER	ISSUED TO	DEPOSIT	WITHDRAWAL	BALANCE
						$376.80
13.	____	____	_____	____	____	____
14.	____	____	_____	____	____	____
15.	____	____	_____	____	____	____
16.	____	____	_____	____	____	____
17.					Service Charge	_____
18.					New Balance	_____

Write About It

19. What reasons are there for having a checking account? Write a paragraph including situations in which you would prefer to write a check rather than pay cash.

_____

_____

_____

◢4•2 Reconciling a Bank Statement

◢**IN THIS LESSON, YOU WILL LEARN**

To compare and adjust a personal check register to agree with a monthly bank statement

WORDS TO LEARN

Bank statement *a report of all transactions and the balance in an account*

Opening balance *the amount in an account at the beginning date of a bank statement*

Closing balance *the amount in an account at the end date of a bank statement*

Overdrawn account *an account in which a check is written for more money than the account balance*

Reconcile *to match the information in the check register with the transactions shown for the account on the bank statement*

Robert's check register shows a deposit of $150, but he does not remember when he made the deposit. Robert needs to pay his electric and telephone bills. He wants to make sure that his account will not be overdrawn. How can he find out the dates of his checking account transactions for this month?

New Idea

A **bank statement** (bank STAYT-muhnt) shows all the transactions for one month. The **opening balance** (OH-puhn-ihng BA-luhns) is the amount in an account at the beginning date of a bank statement. The **closing balance** (KLOHZ-ihng BA-luhns) is the amount in an account at the end date of a bank statement. An **overdrawn account** (oh-ver-DRAWN uh-KOWNT) is an account in which a check is written for more money than there is in the account when the check reaches the bank for payment.

Example: Where can Robert look to find out the dates of his checking account transactions? Robert can look at his monthly bank statement to find the dates of his checking account transactions.

Robert Jones		**SOLDIERS BANK**			Statement Period	
111 Mark St.					12-01 to 12-31	
New York, NY 10000					Opening Balance: $356.00	
Account #: 123-456						

TRANSACTION ACTIVITY

DATE	CHECK #	WITHDRAWAL (−)	DEPOSIT (+)	FEE (−)	BALANCE
12/03	398	$ 5.00			$351.00
12/06	394	58.90			292.10
12/06			$150.00		442.10
12/15	395	125.00			317.10
12/31	397	35.00			282.10
12/31				2.50	279.60
			Closing Balance:		$279.60

From the statement, Robert can see which checks have been cashed. He also can see that the $150 deposit was made on 12/06. The check numbers are listed in the order in which the bank received them.

 ## Focus on the Idea

A monthly bank statement for a checking account shows the balance in the account, which checks have been cashed, and how much money has been deposited into the account.

Practice

Use the bank statement above to answer exercises 1 to 3. Part of the first one has been done for you.

1. Which amount is greater, the opening balance or the closing balance? How much greater? __opening balance;__

2. How many checks were deducted from Robert's account for this month? _____

3. What is the total amount recorded this month for withdrawals? _____

Extend the Idea

It is important to **reconcile** (REK-on-seyel), or match the information in the check register, with the transactions listed on the bank statement every month. Here is part of Robert's check register.

DATE	CHECK #	ISSUED TO	DEPOSIT	WITHDRAWAL	BALANCE
					$356.00
12/01	394	Telephone Co.		$58.90	297.10
12/01	395	Harry Smith		125.00	172.10
12/06			$150.00		322.10
12/10	396	Music City		24.75	297.35
12/14	397	School Store		35.00	262.35
12/18	398	Clothes Studio		5.00	$257.35

Example: To reconcile Robert's check register against the bank statement, follow these steps.

Step 1 Compare the checks in the register with those that the bank has cashed.

Check #396, $24.75, appears in register only.

Step 2 List any deposits that have not yet been recorded. Robert's deposit in his register has been recorded in his bank statement.

Step 3 Subtract all fees listed on the bank statement from the check register balance.

$257.35 − $2.50 = $254.85.

Step 4 Adjust the statement balance by subtracting withdrawals and adding deposits listed in the register but not in the statement.

$279.60 − $24.75 = $254.85

Step 5 Be sure that this adjusted bank statement balance matches Robert's adjusted register balance.

✓ Check the Math

4. Pete's bank statement had a closing balance of $125.95. His check register showed a balance of $95. Pete noticed that a check for $30.95 was not included on his bank statement. He was sure that his register balance was correct. Was he right? Why or why not?

_____

_____

Practice

Determine if each register balance is correct. Then, either write correct or, if it is incorrect, write the actual balance. The first one is done for you.

	Bank Statement Closing Balance	Checks not included in Bank Statement	Register Balance	Correct/ Actual Balance
5.	$165.50	$32.00	$197.50	$133.50
6.	$975.00	$21.40, $231.00	$722.60	_____
7.	$1,564.00	$123.85, $65.00	$1,440.35	_____
8.	$278.75	$23.65, $65.50	$189.60	_____

Apply the Idea

Use Maria Ruiz's First Royalty Bank statement to fill in her check register. Then use the statement for exercises 18 to 20.

Maria Ruiz 23 Main St. New York, NY 10000 Account #: 333-333		**FIRST ROYALTY BANK**		Statement Period 11-01-95 to 11-31-95 Opening Balance: $578		

TRANSACTION ACTIVITY

DATE	CHECK #	WITHDRAWAL	DEPOSIT	FEE	BALANCE
11/03	452	$32.75			$545.25
11/06	454	125.00			420.25
11/07			$110.00		530.25
11/15			150.00		680.25
11/20	457	15.75			664.50
11/30	455	200.00			464.50
				$4.50	460.00
				Closing Balance:	$460.00

	Date	Check #	Issued To	Deposit	Withdrawal	Balance
						$578.00
9.	11/01	452	Jerry Grath		$32.75	_____
10.	11/04	453	Telephone Co.		78.80	_____
11.	11/05	454	Super Foods		125.00	_____
12.	11/07			$110.00		_____
13.	11/10	455	Bev's Boutique		200.00	_____
14.	11/15			$150.00		_____
15.	11/17	456	Cash		100.00	_____
16.	11/18	457	Bookstore		15.75	_____
17.	11/30		(fee)		4.50	_____

18. Which checks that Maria wrote have not appeared in the bank statement? _____

19. What is the total amount of these checks? _____

20. Is Maria's check record correct? Use your answer to exercise 19 and the bank statement to find out. _____

Write About It

21. Write a paragraph telling whether or not you think it would be important for you to compare your check register to a monthly bank statement. Explain your reasons.

_____

_____

4•3 Using a Savings Account

Jackie has a savings account that pays interest. Her bank has just raised the interest rates on savings accounts. How can she find out how much interest she has already earned?

New Idea

A **savings account** (SAY-vihngs uh-KOWNT) is a bank account on which interest is paid. A **passbook** (PAS-book) shows the dates and amounts of withdrawals and deposits and the balances. It also shows how much interest was earned. **Interest** (IHN-trihst) is the money the bank pays on deposited money. It is usually a percentage of the average balance in the account.

Example: How much interest has Jackie earned?

Jackie can check her savings account passbook to find out how much interest she has earned.

Date	Interest	Withdrawal	Deposit	Balance
				$254.49
10/03	—	$200.00	—	54.49
10/03	$.45	—	—	54.94
10/25	—	—	$450.00	504.94
11/03	$.25	—	—	$505.19

Jackie has earned $.70 interest.

✓Check Your Understanding

1. How often does the bank pay interest on Jackie's savings account? _____

Focus on the Idea

A savings account passbook shows the transactions, interest, and balance in the account.

Practice

Use Jackie's passbook to answer the following.

2. When will the next interest payment be? _____
3. How much did Jackie deposit in October? _____
4. How much money did she withdraw in October? _____
5. How was the balance of $54.94 on 10/03 determined?

   _____

6. What will Jackie's balance be if she withdraws $200 on 11/04? _____

Apply the Idea

Use Jamal's passbook shown below to answer exercises 7 to 10.

Date	Interest	Withdrawal	Deposit	Balance
				$675.00
9/01	$1.69			$676.69
9/02		$245.00		431.69
9/13		100.00		331.69
10/01	.83			332.52
10/05			$450.00	782.52
11/01	1.95			$784.47

7. What was Jamal's balance before his September interest payment? _____
8. How much interest did Jamal earn from 9/01 through 11/01?
   _____
9. How much were Jamal's withdrawals? _____
10. If Jamal deposits $150 on 11/02, what will his new balance be? _____

Write About It

11. Write a paragraph explaining how interest paid on a savings account affects the balance.

   _____

   _____

   _____

4•4 Finding Simple Interest

IN THIS LESSON, YOU WILL LEARN

To calculate simple interest on a loan balance

WORDS TO LEARN

Simple interest *interest paid at the end of a time period (usually a year)*

Principal *total amount of money on which interest is paid*

Holder's Bank pays a 3% annual rate of interest on the amount of money in a savings account. Ed had $450 in his account last year. How much interest did he earn?

New Idea

Interest that is paid at the end of a time period is **simple interest** (SIHM-puhl IHN-trihst). The total amount of money on which interest is paid is the **principal** (PRIHN-sih-puhl). To find simple interest (I), banks multiply the principal (p) times the rate (r) times the time (t). This is expressed by the formula $I = prt$.

To find Ed's interest, follow these steps.

Step 1   Express the rate of interest as a decimal.

$3\% = 0.03.$ ← Move the decimal point two places left.

Step 2   Use the formula: $I = prt$.
Time is expressed in years, so substitute 1 for t.
$I = \$450 \times 0.03 \times 1 = \$13.50$

Ed earned $13.50 interest last year.

Remember

To round money to the nearest cent, look at the digit in the thousandths place. If it is 5 or greater, add 1 to the digit. If it is less than 5, do not change the digit. Just drop all digits to the right of that place.

$1.146 rounds to $1.15. $1.143 rounds to $1.14.

Focus on the Idea

To find simple interest, first express the annual rate of interest as a decimal. Then use the formula I = prt.

Practice

Change each percent to a decimal. The first two are done for you.

1. 45% ___0.45___
2. 125% ___1.25___
3. 1% _____
4. 56% _____
5. 200% _____
6. 3% _____
7. 5.4% _____
8. 75.5% _____
9. 13% _____
10. 0.5% _____
11. 0.04% _____
12. 7.05% _____

Round each amount to the nearest cent.

13. $13.456 _____
14. $124.672 _____
15. $2.543 _____
16. $.345 _____
17. $1.1234 _____
18. $35.999 _____

Complete the chart. (Annual interest rate means that *t* = 1.)

	Balance	Annual Interest Rate	Amount of Annual Interest
19.	$500	6%	_____
20.	$125	3.2%	_____
21.	$255.50	12%	_____
22.	$32	2%	_____
23.	$1,575	1.5%	_____
24.	$10,568	3.05%	_____

Apply the Idea

25. Jason's bank pays 4% simple interest yearly. Jason deposited $750 in a savings account. How much interest did he earn in one year? How much interest did he earn in one month?

   _____

26. Suppose you deposit $1,200 in a savings account and leave it for a year. If the bank's annual interest rate is 3.5%, how much will be in the account at the end of the year?

   _____

Write About It

27. Choose ten terms from Chapter 4. Use another piece of paper to define these terms and give examples of them, using your own words.

4•5 Finding Compound Interest

In this lesson, you will learn

To calculate interest compounded annually, quarterly, and monthly

Words to learn

Quarterly *every 3 months, or 4 times per year*

Compound interest *interest paid on both the principal and the accumulated interest*

On money held in savings accounts, Central Bank pays 3% annual interest compounded **quarterly** (KWAR-ter-lee). That means it pays 3% interest four times per year, or every three months. If Jan deposits $1,000 for a year, what will her balance be at the end of the year?

New Idea

Compound interest (KOM-pownd IHN-trihst) is interest that is paid on the principal and the accumulated interest. To calculate compound interest, you need to add the interest earned to the principal, and then find the interest on each new balance.

Example: Find the interest on $1,000 at 3% annual rate compounded quarterly.

Add the interest for each quarter to the balance at the end of each quarter. Use the same formula you used to find simple interest, $I = prt$, or $prt = I$.

In this case, time is one quarter, $\frac{1}{4}$, or 0.25, of 1 year.

Quarter	Principal	×	Rate	×	Time	=	Interest		
1st	$1,000.00	×	0.03	×	0.25	=	$7.50		
	$1,000.00			+			$7.50	=	$1,007.50
2nd	$1,007.50	×	0.03	×	0.25	=	$7.56 (rounded)		
	$1,007.50			+			$7.56	=	$1,015.06
3rd	$1,015.06	×	0.03	×	0.25	=	$7.61 (rounded)		
	$1,015.06			+			$7.61	=	$1,022.67
4th	$1,022.67	×	0.03	×	0.25	=	$7.67		
	$1,022.67			+			$7.67	=	$1,030.34
			(balance after four quarters, twelve months, or 1 year)						

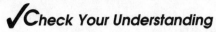

1. Suppose you want to open a savings account. Would you go to a bank that pays 3% annual simple interest or to one that pays 3% annual interest compounded quarterly? Explain your answer.

_____

_____

_____

Focus on the Idea

To find compound interest, first find the interest paid at the end of the first interest period and add that amount to the balance. Repeat this process for the number of periods the interest is compounded.

Practice

Suppose an annual interest rate of 4% is compounded monthly on an account that had $600 deposited into it on January 1. (One month is about 0.08 of a year.) Complete the chart to find the balance in the account after three months.

2. 2/1 **interest:** $600.00 × 0.04 × 0.08 = _____

   new balance: _____ + _____ = _____

3. 3/1 **interest:** _____ × 0.04 × 0.08 = _____

   new balance: _____ + _____ = _____

4. 4/1 **interest:** _____ × 0.04 × 0.08 = _____

   new balance: _____ + _____ = _____

5. How much will Alice's balance be if she keeps $750 in a savings account for 1 year, at 3.5% compounded quarterly?

   _____

6. Which savings account pays more on $1,000 after 1 year? How much more?

   a. Savings Account 1: 4% annually, simple interest

   b. Savings Account 2: 3.5% annually, compounded quarterly

   _____

   _____

Extend the Idea

Banks offer several kinds of savings programs. Here are three kinds offered by one bank:

Certificate of Deposit (CD)

        6-month CD: 3.6% annual interest
        1-year CD: 4.3% annual interest
        3-year CD: 5% annual interest

Money Market Account

        Annual interest of 3.6% compounded quarterly (every 3 months)

Savings Account

        Annual interest of 3.6% compounded monthly

Suppose you have $500 to save for six months. You can find out which account would pay you the most interest by calculating how much would be in each type of account after six months.

✓Check the Math

7. To find the interest paid on a 6-month CD, should you use 0.5 as the "time" in the interest formula? Why or why not?

Practice

Which rate and method of compounding interest, *a* or *b*, would pay the greater amount? How much more would it pay?

8. $1,500 saved for 1 year at an annual interest of
   a. 4% compounded quarterly
   b. 4.2% compounded semi-annually, or two times a year

   ---

9. $2,000 saved for 3 years at an annual interest of
   a. 3% compounded semi-annually
   b. 3.5% compounded annually

   ---

10. $450 saved for 3 months at an annual interest of
    a. 5% compounded quarterly
    b. 4.8% compounded monthly

    ---

11. $3,500 saved for $2\frac{1}{2}$ years at an annual interest of
    a. 6% compounded semi-annually, or two times a year
    b. 4.5% compounded quarterly

Apply the Idea

12. Which kind of account described in "Extend the Idea" would pay the most interest on $500 after six months? How much would you have after six months if you put $500 into this account? _____

13. How much more interest would you earn by saving $1,000 in the 1-year CD than saving $1,000 in the money market account for one year? _____

✎ Write About It

14. Write a paragraph explaining the main differences between simple interest and compound interest.

_____

_____

_____

15. Choose three local banks. Find out the different types of CDs each bank offers and the interest paid by each. Use the chart to compare the differences among the banks. Display the charts. Compare your information with the information found by others in your class.

Bank: _____		**Bank:** _____		**Bank:** _____	
Type of CD	**Interest paid**	**Type of CD**	**Interest paid**	**Type of CD**	**Interest paid**
1. _____ _____		1. _____ _____		1. _____ _____	
2. _____ _____		2. _____ _____		2. _____ _____	
3. _____ _____		3. _____ _____		3. _____ _____	

◢4•6 Borrowing Money

◢ IN THIS LESSON, YOU WILL LEARN

To calculate fixed and variable interest rates on loans

WORDS TO LEARN

Loan *money borrowed*

Fixed interest rate *a rate of interest that does not change for the length of the loan*

Variable interest rate *a rate of interest that changes or varies during the loan period*

Cap *the highest interest rate that can be charged on a variable loan*

Sharon decided to borrow $1,000 from her bank. The chart below describes two loan plans for a $1,000 principal. Which plan should she choose?

	Principal	Annual Interest Rate	Type of Rate	Length of Loan
Plan A	$1,000	12%	Fixed	2 years
Plan B	$1,000	10% 1st year; cap of up to 3% more for 2nd year	Variable	2 years

New Idea

When you borrow money, you repay the amount of your **loan** (lohn) along with a percent of that amount, as interest. A **fixed interest rate** (fihkst IHN-trihst rayt) does not change for the length of the loan. A **variable interest rate** (VAIR-ee-uh-buhl IHN-trihst rayt) is an interest rate that may or may not change during a loan period.

Which plan charges less interest over two years?

Plan A

Use the formula for finding simple interest.

Principal × Rate × Time = Interest
$1,000 × 0.12 × 2 = $240

Sharon would pay $240 in interest with Plan A.

Plan B

Step 1 Find simple interest for the 1st year.
$1,000 × 0.10 × 1 = $100

Step 2 Find the highest possible interest rate for the 2nd year. Since the 1st year's rate is 10% and the maximum increase, or **cap**, is 3%, the highest possible interest rate for the 2nd year is 13% (10% + 3%).

Step 3   Find the highest possible interest to be paid for the 2nd year. $1,000 × 13% × 1 = $130

Step 4   Add the interest for 2 years. $100 + $130 = $230

Sharon would pay $230 or less in interest with Plan B. Plan B charges the lower amount of interest.

Focus on the Idea

To find fixed interest, use the interest formula, prt = I. To find variable interest, use the same formula but use the highest interest rate possible.

Practice

Complete the chart to find the highest interest rate possible. The first one has been done for you.

	Variable Interest Rate	Increase	Highest Rate (Cap)
1.	13.6%	4.0%	17.6%
2.	3.5%	4.2%	_____
3.	23.0%	2.75%	_____
4.	9.0%	3.5%	_____
5.	12.75%	2.75%	_____

Apply the Idea

6. Jack borrowed $1,500 at a fixed rate of 10% per year for 2 years. Meg borrowed $1,200 at a variable rate of 10% for the first year and a cap of 5% more for the second year.

   a. How much interest will Jack pay in all? _____

   b. What is the most interest Meg will pay? _____

   c. Who is paying a higher interest rate? How can you tell?

   _____

Write About It

7. Tell why a borrower might choose a loan plan with a fixed interest rate over one with a variable interest rate. Why would a borrower choose a variable rate over a fixed rate?

   _____

   _____

   _____

4•7 Comparing Loan Repayment Plans

IN THIS LESSON, YOU WILL LEARN

To calculate and compare the costs of monthly loan payments

WORDS TO LEARN

Available funds *income remaining after all expenses have been paid*

Stan needs to borrow $1,500. He earns $900 per month. His total expenses are $775 per month. Which loan plan is better for Stan?

Loan Plan A	*Loan Plan B*
Amount Borrowed: $1,500	Amount Borrowed: $1,500
Interest Rate: 12% per year	Interest Rate: 10%
Length of Loan: 3 years	Length of Loan: 1 year
(36 monthly payments)	(12 monthly payments)

New Idea

A monthly payment is the amount paid to the bank each month to repay a loan. To calculate monthly payments, find the total amount to be paid, including interest; then divide by the number of payments.

Example: Which loan plan, A or B, is better for Stan?

		Loan Plan A	Loan Plan B
Step 1	He finds the total to be paid to the bank including interest.	$1,500 × 0.12 × 3 = $540 $1,500 + $540 = $2,040	$1,500 × 0.10 × 1 = 150 $1,500 + $150 = $1,650
Step 2	He divides the total amount repaid by the number of monthly payments.	$2,040 ÷ 36 = $56.67	$1,650 ÷ 12 = $137.50

For Plan A, Stan would pay $56.67 each month for 36 months. For Plan B, his payments would be $137.50 each month for 12 months.

Stan must decide which plan better fits his budget. He figures his **available funds**, or the amount remaining each month after expenses.

Income	–	Expenses	=	Available Funds
$900	–	$775	=	$125

Then Stan compares the monthly payments for each plan to his available funds. Stan decides that Loan Plan A is better for him.

Focus on the Idea

To calculate the amount of monthly loan payments, find the amount of interest and the total amount to be repaid. Then divide by the number of payments.

Practice

Find the amount of each person's monthly available funds. The first one has been done for you.

	Person	Monthly Income	Monthly Expenses	Available Funds
1.	Keisha	$2,700.00	$2,459.00	<u>$241</u> per month
2.	Trevor	$ 975.75	$ 842.00	_____ per month
3.	Sam	$1,095.00	$ 989.50	_____ per month
4.	Adam	$ 650.00	$ 597.00	_____ per month

Complete the chart. Round all answers to the nearest hundredth or cent. The first one has been started.

	Principal p	Rate r	Time t	Interest $I = prt$	Total Amount $I + p$	Monthly Payment $(I + p) \div$ *number of months*
5.	$1,400	0.03	2 y	<u>$84</u>	<u>$1,484</u>	_____
6.	$575	0.15	3 y	_____	_____	_____
7.	$2,500	0.125	5 y	_____	_____	_____
8.	$12,500	0.06	15 y	_____	_____	_____

Apply the Idea

9. Jamal earns $1,450 per month. His monthly expenses total $1,339. Jamal wants to borrow $2,400. Could he afford to borrow it from a bank that offers $2,400 at 11.5% annual interest for 4 years? Explain why or why not.

_____

Write About It

10. What are some advantages of taking out a loan for a longer period of time? What are some disadvantages?

_____

Chapter 4   Review

In This Chapter, You Have Learned
- To write checks and balance a checking account
- To compare and adjust a personal record
- To understand how to use a passbook savings account
- To calculate simple, fixed, or variable interest on a loan
- To calculate annual, quarterly, and monthly interest
- To calculate monthly loan payments

Words You Know

Write the letter of the phrase in column 2 that defines each word in column 1.

Column 1	Column 2
1. deposit _____	a. amount on which interest is paid
2. withdrawal _____	b. money remaining in an account
3. balance _____	c. to put money into an account
4. interest _____	d. limit put on the rate of interest
5. transaction _____	e. any activity in an account
6. passbook _____	f. record of savings account transactions
7. principal _____	g. amount of money taken out of an account
8. cap _____	h. money the bank pays to depositors

More Practice

Complete the check register.

	DATE	CHECK NUMBER	ISSUED TO	DEPOSIT	WITHDRAWAL	BALANCE
						$127.65
9.	6/01	456	J.P. Smith		$45.75	_____
10.	6/07			$53.45		_____
11.	6/15	457	Cash		98.50	_____

Adjust the check register balance to agree with the bank statement's closing balance and checks not yet included.

	Bank Statement Closing Balance	Checks not included in bank statement	Register Balance
12.	$178.65	$13.55; $15.50	_____
13.	$758	$123.75; $72.50	_____
14.	$250	$24.00; $21; $15.60	_____

Complete the chart to find the annual interest for each balance.

	Balance	Annual Interest Rate	Annual Interest
15.	$875	5%	_____
16.	$1,250	4.2%	_____

Annual interest of 5% is compounded monthly on a deposit of $800. One month is about 0.08 of a year. Complete the chart.

		Interest	Balance
17.	March 1	$800 $\times 0.05 \times 0.08 =$ _____;	$800 + ____ =$ _____
18.	April 1	_____ $\times 0.05 \times 0.08 =$ _____;	____ $+$ ___ $=$ _____

Complete the chart to find the highest possible interest rate to be paid for the 2nd year.

	Variable Interest Rate for First Year	Increase	Highest Rate of Interest (Cap)
19.	9%	3% cap	_____
20.	10%	2.5% cap	_____

Complete the chart.

	Amount Borrowed	Interest Rate	Length of Loan	Interest Paid	Total Paid	Monthly Payments
21.	$1,500	8%	3 y	_____	_____	_____
22.	$ 850	12.5%	5 y	_____	_____	_____

Problems You Can Solve

23. Megan's bank pays 3% annual interest compounded quarterly. If Megan deposits $1,500 on January 1st, how much will she have at the end of the year? _____

24. Mr. Montino had a balance of $24,780 in his checking account. He deposited $2,000 more. Then he wrote checks for $15,000 for college tuition and $2,000 for a new computer. After writing these checks, what was Mr. Montino's balance? _____

25. For Your Portfolio Write a problem based on the information on the sign on page 55. Exchange your problem with a classmate. Then solve each other's problems.

_____

_____

_____

Chapter 4   Practice Test

Complete this check register.

	Date	Check Number	Issued To	Deposit	Withdrawal	Balance
						$117.82
1.	2/24	102	J.C. Electric	—	$35.85	_____
2.	2/27	—	—	$45.00	—	_____

Balance the check register so that it agrees with the bank statement's closing balance and checks that were not included.

	Bank Statement Closing Balance	Checks Not Included In Bank Statement	Register Balance
3.	$265.30	$10.50 ; $12.75	_____
4.	$1,007.00	$125.00 ; $11.00 ; $75.40	_____

Complete the chart to find the amount of annual interest.

	Balance	Annual Interest Rate	Annual Interest
5.	$925	15%	_____
6.	$1,450.00	5.5%	_____

Complete the chart to find the highest possible interest in the 2nd year.

	Variable Interest Rate for First Year	Increase	Highest Rate of Interest (Cap)
7.	8%	4.5% cap	_____
8.	11%	2.2% cap	_____

Complete the chart.

	Amount Borrowed	Interest Rate	Length of Loan	Interest Paid	Total Paid	Monthly Payments
9.	$1,800	9.5%	3 y	_____	_____	_____

10. Beth borrowed $1,500 for three years at an annual interest rate of 6.5%. Carey borrowed $1,500 from another bank for five years at an annual interest rate of 5%.

   a. Whose monthly payments are higher, and by how much?

   _____

   b. Who will pay more total interest? How much more?

   _____

Chapter 5

Becoming an Informed Shopper

OBJECTIVES:

In this chapter, you will learn

- *To uncover and evaluate hidden costs*
- *To find the price of a sale item*
- *To determine the total cost of buying something from a catalog*
- *To evaluate information given in ads*
- *To determine the total cost of something advertised as being "on sale"*

Ramón wants a radio with headphones and batteries. The chart tells the prices of the same radio on sale in two different stores. In this chapter, you will learn how Ramón can decide on the better buy.

	M&M Electronics	**B&B's Sound Store**
Product	AM/FM Radio with headphone (requires 2 AA batteries)	AM/FM Radio (requires headphones and 2 AA batteries)
Regular Price	$25.95	$19.95
Rate of Discount	15% off	$\frac{1}{3}$ off
Hidden Costs	Batteries: package of 2 AA for $2.29	Headphones: $9.99 Batteries: package of 2 AA for $1.99

◀5•1 Recognizing Hidden Costs

◀ IN THIS LESSON, YOU WILL LEARN

To uncover and evaluate hidden costs

WORDS TO LEARN

Regular price *the price of an item as suggested by the manufacturer*

Hidden cost *the cost of something you need to have in order to use another item*

Total cost *the regular price of an item plus any hidden costs*

Carlos and his sister are shopping for a CD player as a present for their parents. What hidden cost is involved in buying this CD player? What is the total cost of the CD player, including the hidden cost?

Portable CD Player $129.00	Batteries
Requires 4 D batteries Batteries not included	4 AA batteries for $2.49 2 C batteries for $2.29 2 D batteries for $2.49

New Idea

The price you pay for something you buy is the **regular price** (REHG-yuh-luhr prys). If you must buy something else in order for the original item to work, the cost of this is called a **hidden cost** (HIHD-uhn kawst). In this case, the CD player cannot be used without 4 D-size batteries. These are not included in the price.

To find the **total cost** (TOHT-uhl kawst), add the hidden cost (the price of the batteries) to the regular price.

You can estimate the total cost to get an idea of how much you will need to pay. One package of 2 D-size batteries costs $2.49, which is about $2.50. You need two packages. Estimate: 2 • $2.50 = $5.00

Estimate the cost of the CD player plus batteries.

Estimated total cost: $130 + $5 = $135

To figure the exact cost of the CD player, including the hidden cost:

2 • $2.49 = $4.98 Total hidden cost

$129.00 + $4.98 = $133.98 Total cost

⤳Remember

Check your estimate against your exact answer to make sure your exact answer is reasonable.

Focus on the Idea

To find the total cost of something, always add the hidden costs to the regular price.

Practice

Estimate. Then find the exact total cost of each item. Compare each estimate to the exact cost. The first one has been done for you. Follow the order of operations: multiply first, then add.

	Regular Price	Hidden Costs	Estimate Total Cost	Exact Total Cost
1.	$24.75	3 × $4.50	3 × 5 = $15 $25 + $15 = $40	3 × $4.50 = $13.50 $24.75 + $13.50 = $38.25
2.	$87.50	2 × $7.25		
3.	$52.70	5 × $3.89		

Apply the Idea

	REX Cassette Recorder	Aleo Cassette Recorder
Regular Price	$29.99	$39.99
Headphones	$10.99	$12.99
Batteries	2 C for $2.59	4 AA for $2.99

4. Hank has $62 to buy a cassette recorder, batteries, and headphones.

   a. Estimate the actual total cost of each recorder, including hidden costs. _____

   b. Find the actual total cost of each recorder. Remember to add all hidden costs. _____

   c. Can Hank buy either one of the cassette recorders? Explain.

   _____

Write About It

5. Why is it important to find the hidden costs for something you plan to buy? Explain your answer.

   _____

   _____

◢5•2 Understanding Discounts and Sales

◢**IN THIS LESSON, YOU WILL LEARN**

To find the price of a sale item

WORDS TO LEARN

Sale price *the price of an item at less than the regular price*

Amount of discount *how much is subtracted from the regular price*

Rate of discount *a fraction or a percent of the regular price*

SKATE CITY
20% off regular price
of all in-line skates

HI FLYERS
Regular price: $75

ROLLER MADNESS
10% off
regular prices

HI FLYERS
Regular price: $68

Hi Flyers are on sale at a discounted price at each store.
Which store has the lower price?

New Idea

The regular price of Hi Flyers is $75 at Skate City and $68 at Roller Madness. Now, the skates are on sale.

The **sale price** (sayl prys) of an item is less than the regular price. Use these steps to find the sale price if the rate of discount is given as a percent.

Step 1   Find the **amount of discount** (uh-MOUWNT uhv DIHS-kownt), which is how much you can subtract from the regular price. Do this by multiplying the **rate of discount** (rayt uhv DIHS-kownt), a fraction or percent of the regular price, by the regular price.

Regular Price • Rate of Discount = Amount of Discount

Step 2   Find the sale price. Subtract the amount of discount from the regular price.

Regular Price − Amount of Discount = Sale Price

Examples: Which store, Skate City or Roller Madness, has the lower price for Hi Flyers?

Skate City	Roller Madness
$75 • 0.20 = $15	$68 • 0.10 = $6.80
(Amount of discount)	(Amount of discount)
Skate City	Roller Madness
$75 − $15 = $60	$68 − $6.80 = $61.20
(Sale price)	(Sale price)

The regular price of Hi Flyers is lower at Roller Madness, but the sale price is lower at Skate City.

 Check the Math

1. Bill knew that Skate City and Roller Madness sold Hi Flyers. He decided to buy a pair at Sports Center. There, the skates were on sale for 25% off the regular price of $84. Did Bill get the lowest price? Why or why not?

_____

_____

Focus on the Idea

To find the sale price, follow these two steps:
Step 1   Find the amount of discount.

Regular Price • Discount Rate = Discount Amount

Step 2   Find the sale price.

Regular Price − Discount Amount = Sale Price

Practice

Find the amount of the discount and the sale price. When necessary, round answers to the nearest cent. The first one is done for you.

	Item	Regular Price	Rate of Discount	Amount of Discount	Sale Price
2.	Shoes	$62	3%	$62 × 0.03 = $1.86	$62.00 − $1.86 = $60.14
3.	Coat	$125	12.5%	_____	_____
4.	Sweater	$45.75	25%	_____	_____
5.	Gloves	$12	5.5%	_____	_____

Find the amount of discount and the sale price.

6. Regular price: $500
   Rate of discount: 25%

   Amount of discount: _____

   Sale price: _____

7. Regular price: $185
   Rate of discount: 15%

   Amount of discount: _____

   Sale price: _____

Extend the Idea

Sometimes a discount is written as a fraction.
The jewelry is on sale for $\frac{1}{4}$ off the regular price.
Use these steps to find the amount of discount when
the rate of discount is given as a fraction.

Step 1   Change the fraction to a decimal by dividing the
numerator by the denominator.

$$\frac{\text{numerator}}{\text{denominator}} \rightarrow \frac{1}{4} = 4\overline{)1.00}^{\,0.25} \text{ so } \frac{1}{4} = 0.25$$

**Remember**

You can change the decimal 0.25 to a percent by moving the
decimal point two places to the right to express the rate of discount as
a percent (0.25 = 25%).

Step 2   Find the amount of discount and sale price as before.

$48 Regular Price • 0.25 Rate of Discount = $12 Amount of Discount

$48 Regular Price − $12 Amount of Discount = $36 Sale Price

✓Check Your Understanding

8. Change $\frac{1}{8}$ to a decimal. Round your answer to the nearest
   hundredth. _____

9. Change $\frac{1}{8}$ to a percent. _____

Practice

**Rewrite each fraction as a percent. Round to the nearest whole
percent. The first one has been done for you.**

10. $\frac{1}{5} =$ _0.20 = 20%_

11. $\frac{1}{3} =$ _____

12. $\frac{2}{5} =$ _____

13. $\frac{1}{2} =$ _____

14. $\frac{2}{3} =$ _____

15. $\frac{3}{4} =$ _____

Find the amount of discount. The first one has been done for you.

16. $\frac{1}{4}$ off $56 $56 \cdot 0.25 = $14   **17.** $\frac{1}{3}$ off $69 _____

18. $\frac{1}{2}$ off $67 _____   **19.** $\frac{2}{5}$ off $97 _____

Apply the Idea

20. Leather jackets are on sale at $\frac{1}{3}$ off the regular price of $375. How much does a jacket cost on sale? _____

21. A pair of $45 blue jeans is on sale for 15% off. A $38 pair is on sale for 10% off. Which jeans have a lower sale price? How much are these jeans? _____

Use the following store ads to answer questions 22 to 24.

22. A backpack at School Daze originally cost $45. What is its sale price? _____

23. What is the sale price of the backpack that costs the most at Lee's? _____

24. At which store can you buy the backpack with the lower sale price? What is that sale price?

_____

✎ Write About It

25. Sometimes the rate of discount is given as a percent. Other times, it is given as a fraction. Explain the differences. Which way makes it easier for you to understand the rate of discount? Why?

_____

_____

_____

◢ **IN THIS LESSON, YOU WILL LEARN**

To determine the total cost of buying something from a catalog

WORDS TO LEARN

Merchandise *the products for sale*

Shipping and handling charges *the costs added to the merchandise total for taking an order and mailing it*

Shauna prefers shopping from catalogs to shopping in stores because she is too busy to spend time traveling to the mall. She wants to buy these two gifts from a catalog.

Fold-Up Kite	*Radio Oldies*
This kite folds up to fit into its own carrying pouch. The kite comes in a colorful design and includes a tail and 400-foot line.	You'll love this collection of "oldies but goodies" played on the radio during the 1950s, '60s, and '70s.
No. 1416 Fold-Up Kite $14.75	**No. 6961** *Radio Oldies* **$32.50**

What would be the order total for the Fold-Up Kite and *Radio Oldies?*

New Idea

When ordering **merchandise** (MUR-chuhn-deyz), or items for sale, from a catalog, add to the merchandise total any **shipping and handling charges** (SHIHP-ihng and HAND-lihng CHARJ-uhz) to find your order total. Shipping and handling charges are the extra costs you pay for the catalog company to take your order and mail it.

Example: You can find the order total for the Fold-Up Kite and *Radio Oldies* as follows.

Step 1 Add to find the merchandise total for the two items.

$14.75   Fold-Up Kite

+32.50   *Radio Oldies*

$47.25   Merchandise total

Shipping and Handling Charges	
If merchandise total is:	Add this amount:
Up to $14.99	$2.95
$15.00 – $29.99	$3.95
$30.00 – $39.99	$4.95
$40.00 – $59.99	$5.95
$60.00 or more	$6.95

Step 2 Look at the shipping and handling chart. Find the line that includes the merchandise total you found. Since $47.25 is between $40.00 and $59.99, you must add $5.95 for shipping and handling charges.

$47.25	Merchandise total
+ 5.95	Shipping and handling
$53.20	Order total for Fold-Up Kite and *Radio Oldies*

✓Check the Math

1. Jim ordered three 1,000-piece jigsaw puzzles from the same catalog that listed the Fold-Up Kite and *Radio Oldies*. The merchandise total for the puzzle was $32.97. He calculated his order total to be $37.92. Was he correct? Explain.

_____

_____

_____

◀ Focus on the Idea

To find the order total when shopping from a catalog, add the shipping and handling charges to the merchandise total.

Practice

Use the chart above to find the shipping and handling charges. Then add to find the order total. The first one has been done for you.

	Merchandise Total	Shipping and Handling	Order Total
2.	$65.75	$6.95	$72.70
3.	$34.99	_____	_____
4.	$14.50	_____	_____
5.	$25.00	_____	_____

Extend the Idea

Often, a catalog company will offer special delivery or gift wrapping for an extra charge. You might see this in a catalog:

Extra Services	
Overnight delivery	Add $15.95
Two-day delivery	Add $4.50
Gift wrapping	Add $3.95 per item

Choosing these extra services adds to the total cost of an order. Be sure to include these costs when figuring your order total.

✓Check Your Understanding

6. If you ordered two items from the catalog and wanted them both gift wrapped and delivered overnight, what extra costs would you have? _____

Practice

Use the charts on page 87 and above to find the order total for each order. The first one has been done for you.

	Quantity	Merchandise Total	Shipping and Handling	Extra Services	Order Total
7.	3	$45.00	$5.95	Gift wrap: $3.95 × 3 = $11.85	$45 + $5.95 + $11.85 = $62.80
8.	2	$22.50	_____	2-day delivery: _____	_____
9.	4	$62.75	_____	Gift wrap: _____	_____

Apply the Idea

10. Order four items from those listed. Fill in the order form on page 89. Include at least one extra service in your order.

Beginner's Telescope
Comes with metal tripod and moon and space maps No. B134; $87.75

Global Survival
Business simulation game for ages 13 and up No. B513; $39.95

Astronaut Food
Dehydrated pear, ice cream, and fries (set of 3) No. B345; $9.95

Galaxy Book Set
Set of 5 books about space No. B678; $33.75

Gallivant
Geography board game for ages 13 and up No. B512; $27.00

U.S.S. Enterprise Model
Includes light bulb, wire, and optic fiber to light windows No. B456; $45.00

Shipping and Handling Charges		Extra Service Charges
If merchandise total is:	**Add this amount:**	Gift wrap: add $4 per item
Up to $10.00	$3.50	Overnight delivery: add $12.50
$10.01 – $25.00	$4.50	Two-day delivery: add $5.50
$25.01 – $40.00	$5.75	
$40.01 – $60.00	$7.75	
$60.01 – $100.00	$9.95	
$100.01 and up	$12.50	

Ship and bill to: (Please print)   **ORDER FORM**

Name _____

Address _____

City _____ State ____ Zip _____

Phone (____) _____

Item Number	Quantity	Name of Item	Item Price	Total
_____	_____	_____	_____	_____
_____	_____	_____	_____	_____
_____	_____	_____	_____	_____
_____	_____	_____	_____	_____

MERCHANDISE TOTAL _____

Shipping and Handling _____

Overnight Delivery _____

Gift Wrap _____

Two-Day Delivery _____

ORDER TOTAL _____

✎ Write About It

11. Why might it be worth paying for extra service charges? Describe at least two situations for which you might need these services.

_____

_____

_____

▶5•4 Reading Advertisements

▶ **IN THIS LESSON, YOU WILL LEARN**

To evaluate the information given in ads

To determine the total cost of something advertised as being "on sale"

WORDS TO LEARN

Limit *the greatest number of items that a shopper is allowed to buy at the sale price*

Best buy *the highest quality of merchandise or service available for the least amount of money*

Bonus *an extra item included with a purchase at no additional cost*

MOTO MOTOR OIL
$18.99 per case
12 cans per case

MOTO OIL

Regularly $24.99
Limit: 1 case per customer

AUTO MOTOR OIL

2 days only
20% off regular price
of $25 per case

AUTO MOTOR OIL

12 cans per case

SUPER MOTOR OIL

25% off regular price
of $28 per case

SUPER MOTOR OIL

12 cans per case

What facts do these ads give? What facts about the products are missing? Which product is the best buy?

New Idea

Advertisements give facts about items that merchants want to sell. Most ads tell the name of the product and the sale price. Some ads tell the size of the product and set a **limit** (LIHM-iht), or the most of that item you are allowed to buy at the sale price. To find which motor oil is the **best buy** (behst by), or the one that gives you the most value for your money, compare the prices for equal amounts of each of the three brands.

Each of the ads gives the following information:
- What's on sale: motor oil
- The price: Moto — $18.99; Auto — 20% off $25; Super — 25% off $28
- Limit: Moto — 1 case per customer; Auto — 2 days only

Each ad is missing the following information:
- The size of each can, or the amount of oil it holds
- The weight of the oil

To find out which is the best buy, find the price of equal amounts of each brand of motor oil.

Moto Oil: $18.99 for 12 cans

Auto Oil: $25 • 0.20 = $5 discount
$25 − $5 = $20 for 12 cans

Super Oil: $28 • 0.25 = $7 discount
$28 − $7 = $21 for 12 cans

Twelve cans of Moto Oil cost less than 12 cans of either of the other two brands. Moto Oil is the best buy.

✓ Check the Math

1. Matt needs to buy 2 cases of oil. He decides Moto Oil is the best buy. Is he correct? Explain.

_____

_____

◀ Focus on the Idea

To evaluate ads, think about whether the sale items fit your needs. See if there are any limits. Then determine the price of equal amounts of each product. Compare to see which is the best buy.

Practice

Read the ads below.

Scrubby Soap Powder	Super Clean Detergent	Eco Clean Liquid Detergent
64-oz box for $4.50 Limit: 1 per customer (Additional boxes at $6.99 each)	64-oz box $3.50 off regular price of $7.75 Limit: 2 per customer	64-oz bottle 20% off regular price of $8.50

2. How much does one box of Super Clean Detergent cost?

   _____

3. How much does a bottle of Eco Clean cost?_____

4. If you need only one bottle or box of detergent, which is the best buy and why?

   _____

5. How much would 3 boxes of Scrubby Soap Powder cost?_____

6. How much would 3 boxes of Super Clean cost?_____

7. How much would 3 bottles of Eco Clean cost?_____

Extend the Idea

Sometimes a sale will include a **bonus** (BOH-nuhs), something extra that is free, if you buy the product. Consider the usefulness and amount of the bonus when evaluating the ad. Read these two ads. Find the bonus.

Mr. Drip Coffee Maker
Now through Saturday on Sale:
$62.99
($75 after Saturday)
Bonus: 200 coffee filters ($9.99 value)

Quick Start Coffee Machine
2-Day Sale:
25% off *
* originally $76
Bonus: set of ceramic mugs ($15 value)

✓ Check Your Understanding

8. Which bonus has the greater value? How much greater is its value? _____

Practice

Use the coffee maker ads for exercises 9 to 11.

9. How much does the Quick Start Machine cost on sale?

   _____

10. Which is the better buy, Mr. Drip or Quick Start? Why?

    _____

11. What limits are mentioned in the ads?

    _____

Apply the Idea

OAK BEDROOM PACKAGE
Dresser, Chest of Drawers, Double Headboard, 2 Night Tables All 5 pieces for $699
Bonus: Mirror for Chest (Complete set $959 if items purchased separately)

5-PIECE BEDROOM SET
Dresser, Mirror, Queen-sized Headboard, 2 Night Tables All 5 pieces for $899
*originally $1,199

Read the bedroom-set ads to answer exercises 12 to 14.

12. How do the two bedroom-set packages differ?

    _____

    _____

13. How much would you save if you bought the whole oak bedroom set rather than buying each piece separately?

_____

14. Bill and his wife are moving into a new apartment. They want to buy a new bedroom set. Based on the ads, which is the better buy for them? Why?

_____

_____

Use the following ads to answer these questions.

Mr. E's Electronics
30" TV
$799
Bonus: TV stand

Wally's Warehouse
27" TV
$499
Take an extra 20% off Saturday only

Mr. E's Electronics
27" TV
$100 off original price*
Limit: one per customer
*originally $600

Wally's Warehouse
All 30" TVs on sale
Saturday only
$\frac{1}{3}$ off regular price of $1,299

15. It's Saturday. Where would you buy a 27" TV? Why?

_____

_____

16. It's Saturday. Where would you buy a 30" TV? Why?

_____

_____

17. It's Sunday. Where would you buy a 27" TV? Why?

_____

_____

✏ Write About It

18. Suppose you have a used bike to sell. Write an ad that you can place in your local newspaper to sell your bike.

_____

Chapter 5   Review

In This Chapter, You Have Learned

- To uncover and evaluate hidden costs
- To find the price of a sale item
- To determine the total cost of buying something from a catalog
- To evaluate the information given in ads
- To determine the total cost of something advertised as being "on sale"

Words You Know

From the lists of "Words to Learn," choose the word or phrase that best completes each statement.

1. Randy's Computer Warehouse is having a big sale. All of the _____ is on sale.
2. The _____ is 20% off the _____.
3. When Carol went to buy a computer, there were some _____ for items that did not come with the computer.
4. She had to add these items to the regular price to find the _____ of the computer.

More Practice

Estimate. Then find the exact total cost of each item.

	Regular Price	Hidden Costs	Total Cost Estimate	Exact
5.	$35.75	$7.99 × 2	_____	_____
6.	$59.76	$4.99 and $3.12	_____	_____

Find the amount of the discount and the sale price. Round to the nearest cent when necessary.

	Regular Price	Rate of Discount	Amount of Discount	Sale Price
7.	$56	20%	_____	_____
8.	$125.50	$\frac{1}{3}$	_____	_____
9.	$19.50	15%	_____	_____

Use the shipping and handling charges and extra service charges chart below for exercises 10 and 11.

Total	Shipping and Handling Charges	Extra Service Charges
If merchandise total is: Up to $14.99 $15.00 – $29.99 $30.00 – $39.99 $40.00 – $59.99 $60.00 or more	Add this amount: $2.50 $3.50 $4.50 $5.50 $6.50	Overnight delivery: add $12.95 Two-day delivery: add $5.50 Gift wrap: add $3.50 per item

	Quantity	Merchandise Total	Shipping and Handling	Extra Services	Order Total
10.	2	$38.95	_____	Gift wrap: _____	_____
11.	4	$120.75	_____	Overnight delivery: _____	_____

Problems You Can Solve

Use the ad at the right to answer exercises 12 to 15.

Hair-To-Go Haircutters
Special Tuesdays only Cut and blow dry Men: $12* Women: $12* Children under 12: $7* *$6 off regular prices

12. On Saturday, Mike got his hair cut and dried at Hair-To-Go. How much did he pay? _____

13. On Tuesday, Mrs. Fontaine took her two children, Mary, age 11, and John, age 15, to get their hair cut and dried at Hair-To-Go. Mrs. Fontaine also got a haircut. What was her total bill?

_____

14. On Mondays, how much does Hair-To-Go charge to cut and dry hair for a boy who is 13? _____

15. On Mondays, how much does Hair-To-Go charge to cut and dry hair for a girl who is 13? _____

16. **For Your Portfolio** Work with a partner to decide which radio advertised on page 79 Ramón should buy. Then look in the newspaper for several ads for the same item from different stores. Work with your partner to decide which store has the best buy. Put the information you gather in your portfolio.

Chapter 5 Practice Test

Estimate. Then find the exact total cost of each item.

	Regular Price	Hidden Costs	Total Cost Estimate	Exact
1.	$56.75	$2.99 × 2	_____	_____
2.	$124.69	$1.79 and $3.52	_____	_____

Find the amount of the discount and the sale price. Round to the nearest cent when necessary.

	Regular Price	Rate of Discount	Amount of Discount	Sale Price
3.	$78.50	25%	_____	_____
4.	$19.95	$\frac{1}{5}$	_____	_____

Use the chart below for exercises 5 and 6.

Merchandise Total	Shipping and Handling Charges	Extra Service Charges
Up to $10.99 $11.00 – $24.99 $25.00 – $39.99 $40.00 – $59.99 $60.00 or more	$2.95 $3.95 $5.50 $7.50 $9.50	Overnight delivery: add $14.95 Two-day delivery: add $4.50 Gift wrap: add $3.95 per item

	Quantity	Merchandise Total	Shipping and Handling	Extra Services	Order Total
5.	3	$55.95	_____	Gift wrap: _____	_____
6.	4	$38.59	_____	Overnight delivery: _____	_____

Read the ad at the right. Then answer the questions.

7. How much money will 13-year-old Billy save if he buys an all-day pass on a Friday in May instead of on a Saturday in July? _____

8. How much would a family with 2 adults and 2 children, ages 11 and 12, pay for passes to Adventure Park on a weekday in May? _____

> **Adventure Park**
> Pre-season discount rate*
> (April 1–June 1)
> **_All-day passes_**
> Adults:
> $23.95 Mon.–Thurs.
> $30.00 Fri.–Sun.
> Children 12 and under:
> $17.95 any day
>
> *All prices reflect a $12 discount*

Chapter 6
Making a Purchase

OBJECTIVES:

In this chapter, you will learn

- *To calculate the sales tax and the total cost of an item*
- *To estimate and calculate the amount of change you receive*
- *To find the installment cost for a layaway or an installment purchase*
- *To determine a monthly credit card bill based on monthly interest charged on the unpaid balance*
- *To compare costs of installment buying plans, layaway plans, and credit card account purchases*

ON SALE TODAY ONLY!

State-of-the-Art Camcorder
$989   (regularly $1,050)

Bill wants to buy the camcorder advertised here, but he does not have enough cash right now to pay for it. To take advantage of the sale, he decides to use his credit card to charge the camcorder.

Bill's credit card account charges 22.5% annual interest on the unpaid balance. Bill will pay more for the camcorder if he charges it, but he will be able to use it while he pays for it. Do you think it is a good idea for him to buy the camcorder on credit?

◢6•1 Understanding and Calculating Sales Tax

◢ IN THIS LESSON, YOU WILL LEARN

To calculate the sales tax and the total purchase price of an item

WORDS TO LEARN

Sales tax *a percentage charge added to the price of goods or services purchased*

Purchase price *total of all costs for an item, including sales tax*

Taxable item *an item on which a sales tax is charged*

Non-taxable item *an item on which no sales tax is collected*

State Sales Tax Rates *(Selected States)*							
State	Tax Rate	State	Tax Rate	State	Tax Rate	State	Tax Rate
Alabama	4%	California	6%	Florida	6%	Georgia	4%
Illinois	6.25%	Iowa	5%	New York	4%	Texas	6.25%
Wyoming	4%						

David has $50 to spend on a software program. The price of the program is $47.99. Since David lives in Florida, does he have enough money for the program and the sales tax?

New Idea

Sales tax (saylz taks) is a percentage charge added to the price of goods or services purchased. To find the **purchase price** (PER-chaz preyez), the total of all costs of the program David wants to buy, including sales tax, follow these steps:

Step 1   Find the amount of sales tax charged on the item by multiplying the price of the item times the rate of tax.

⌐Remember

To change a percent to a decimal, drop the percent sign (%) and move the decimal point two places to the left. The tax in Florida, 6%, becomes 0.06.

$$\text{Price} \times \text{Tax Rate} = \text{Amount of Tax}$$
$$\$47.99 \times 0.06 \quad = ?$$
$$\$47.99 \times 0.06 \quad = 2.8794$$
$$\quad = \$2.88 \text{ (rounded to the nearest cent)}$$

Step 2   Find the purchase price by adding the price of the item and the amount of tax.

Price + Amount of Tax = Purchase Price

$47.99 + $2.88   = $50.87

Since the purchase price is $50.87 and David has only $50, he does not have enough money for the program.

✓Check the Math

1. David's cousin lives in Wyoming. She said she bought the same program for less than $50, including tax. Is she correct? Why or why not?

_____

◀ Focus on the Idea

To find the purchase price of an item, including sales tax, use these formulas:
Price × Tax Rate = Amount of Tax
Price + Amount of Tax = Purchase Price

🖩 Practice

For each sale, find the amount of tax and purchase price. Round all answers to the nearest cent. The first one has been done for you.

	Price	Tax Rate	Amount of Tax	Purchase Price
2.	$500	3%	$15	$515
3.	$25.75	4.5%	1.16	26.91
4.	$135	6%	_____	_____
5.	$1,500	8.75%	_____	_____
6.	$15,500	7%	_____	_____

Add each list of prices. Find the amount of sales tax. Then find the purchase price.

7. Maria's Music Store
   Tax rate: 5%

   $ 57.85
   987.65
   213.43
   12.50

   Total cost of items: _____

   Amount of tax: _____

   Purchase price _____

8. JD's Furniture Store
   Tax rate: 7.75%

   $ 105.75
   32.54
   .99
   1,500.00

   Total cost of items: _____

   Amount of tax: _____

   Purchase price _____

Extend the Idea

Different states have different sales tax rates. Different states also charge sales tax on different items. A **taxable item** (TAHKS-uh-buhl EYET-uhm) is one on which a sales tax is collected. A **non-taxable item** (nahn-TAHKS-uh-buhl EYET-uhm) is one on which a sales tax is not collected. When finding the total cost of items you are purchasing, first check to see which items are taxable and which are non-taxable.

Suppose in your state, clothing is a non-taxable item, but sports equipment is a taxable item. The tax rate is 6%. You want to buy the following: blue jeans–$39.95, skates–$75, basketball–$25.75.

What will be your purchase price, including sales tax?

Step 1   First, find the total cost of the non-taxable items:
           Blue jeans $39.95

Step 2   Then, find the total cost of the taxable items:
           Skates $ 75.00
           Basketball   + 25.75
                          $100.75   Cost of taxable items

           Taxable Cost × Tax Rate = Amount of Tax
               $100.75 × 0.06 = $6.05
           Taxable Cost + Amount of Tax = Total Cost of Taxable Items
               $100.75 + $6.05 = $106.80

Step 3   Finally, combine the costs of the non-taxable and taxable items (including tax):
           $39.95 + $106.80 = $146.75   Purchase Price

✓Check Your Understanding

9. Suppose you lived in a state in which the sales tax was 6% and where everything, including clothing, was taxable. How much would your purchase price be for the above items in this state? _____

 Practice

Complete the chart to find each purchase price.

	Cost of Non-Taxable Items	Cost of Taxable Items	Tax Rate	Purchase Price
10.	$125.00	$65.50	7%	_____
11.	$25.00	$49.95	8.75%	_____
12.	$43.50	$179.00	6.5%	_____
13.	$279.85	$1,500.00	8%	_____
14.	$1,450.00	$2,133.00	3%	_____

Find the purchase price for each list of items below. Use these facts.

Taxable: non-food items
Non-taxable: food products
Tax Rate: 5%

15. Ursula's Groceries

Milk	$2.29
Floor wax	1.89
Detergent	3.59
Cheese	2.59

Non-taxable Total: _____

Taxable Total: _____

Amount of Tax: _____

Purchase Price: _____

16. Garcia's Market

Eggs	$1.29
Tomato sauce	1.69
Shampoo	2.29
Pepper	1.89
Mustard	3.99
Batteries	4.29

Non-taxable Total: _____

Taxable Total: _____

Amount of Tax: _____

Purchase Price: _____

Apply the Idea

17. Mark considered buying a car priced at $16,800. He had to pay 6% sales tax on the car in his state.

   a. What would be Mark's purchase price for the car?

   _____

   b. Mark shopped at various dealerships to find the lowest cost for a car with all the features he desires. He found one for $16,250. What is Mark's purchase price for this car? _____

   c. How much did Mark save by shopping around to get the best price? _____

18. Tom lives in a state that has a 5% sales tax on clothing. Sandy lives in a bordering state that does not collect sales tax on clothing. Which would cost less and why?

   a. Buying a winter coat in Tom's state for $159.00

   b. Buying the same winter coat for $169.00 in Sandy's state

   _____

✏ Write About It

19. What is the rate of sales tax in your state? Name at least five kinds of items on which the amount of sales tax alone would be more than $100 if you bought them in your state.

   _____

   _____

6•2 Estimating and Calculating Change

IN THIS LESSON, YOU WILL LEARN

To estimate and calculate the amount of change received

WORDS TO LEARN

Change *the amount of money that is the difference between the cost of an item and the amount used to pay*

Wendy bought the following items at a variety store: a ballpoint pen for $2.79, a notebook for $1.99, and a calculator for $11.20. (The costs listed include tax.) She gave the clerk a $20 bill. How can she estimate how much change she should receive? How can she calculate her exact change?

New Idea

You can estimate the amount of money left over from the amount used to pay for items you buy. This leftover money is called **change** (chaynj). You can estimate your change to determine if the sales clerk gives you back the correct amount of money. An estimate also helps you to see if you will have enough money to buy other things.

To estimate her amount of change, Wendy can round each price to the nearest dollar, then add:

$$\$2.79 \rightarrow \$\ 3$$
$$\$1.99 \rightarrow \ \ 2$$
$$\$11.20 \rightarrow \underline{\ \ 11}$$
$$\$16 \ \ \text{Estimated total cost}$$

She can subtract her estimated total cost from $20:
$$\$20 - \$16 = \$4$$

Four dollars is a good estimate of Wendy's change. To calculate her exact amount of change, Wendy can do the following:

Step 1   Find the total cost of the items:
$$\begin{array}{r} \$\ 2.79 \\ 1.99 \\ +11.20 \\ \hline \$15.98 \end{array} \ \text{Total cost (including tax)}$$

Step 2   Subtract the total cost from the amount paid:

     $20.00   Amount paid
   −15.98   Total cost (including tax)
   $ 4.02   Change

Wendy should receive exactly $4.02 in change.

✓ *Check Your Understanding*

1. Why should you estimate total cost before making a purchase?

   _____

Focus on the Idea

To find about how much change you should receive when making a purchase, first estimate the total cost. Then subtract your estimate from the amount given to the cashier. To find the exact amount of change, add the costs of the items purchased. Then subtract that total from the amount given to the cashier.

Practice

Round the price of each item to estimate the total cost of each purchase to the nearest dollar. Then use pencil and paper to find the exact total. Part of the first one has been done for you.

2. Prices of items	Estimates		3. Prices of items	Estimates
$19.78	$20		$87.54	_____
$23.89	$24		$10.17	_____
$1.20	_____		$9.78	_____
$2.79	_____		$24.59	_____
Estimated Total:	_____		Estimated Total:	_____
Exact Total:	_____		Exact Total:	_____

For each purchase, estimate the amount of change. Then calculate the exact change. The first one has been done for you.

4. Prices of items: $14.95; $28.79; $21.50

   Amount given to cashier: $100

   Estimated change: ___$35___

   Exact change: ___$34.76___

5. Prices of items: $1.89;
$4.68; $8.97; $11.20

Amount given to cashier: $30

Estimated change: _____

Exact change: _____

6. Prices of items: $39.59;
$11.50; $48.99; $.99

Amount given to cashier: $120

Estimated change: _____

Exact change: _____

Extend the Idea

Allison bought a $39.95 sweater, a $48 pair of jeans, and a $66 pair of sneakers. She gave the clerk $160. How much change did she receive?

You can use a calculator to quickly find the exact amount of change due. Here are two different ways to input the information.

Method 1: Start by adding to find the total cost of the items. Record the total in the calculator's memory. Then subtract the total from the amount paid by recalling the total from the memory.

Press: 39.95 **+** 48 **+** 66 **=** **M+** 160 **−** **MR** **=** 6.05

Method 2: Start with the amount given to the clerk. Subtract the cost of each item.

Press: 160 **−** 39.95 **−** 48 **−** 66 **=** 6.05

⤺Remember

M+ adds a number into a calculator's memory. **MR** recalls a number from the memory.

✓Check the Math

7. Allison used Method 1 to calculate her change. She said that 160 is the number that should be saved in the calculator's memory. Is she correct? Why or why not?

_____

🖩 Practice

Find the exact amount of change for each purchase. The first one has been done for you.

8. Prices of items: $14.54; $23.65; $56.32

Amount given to cashier: $100

Exact change: _____$5.49_____

9. Prices of items: $235; $1.87; $34.78; $53.21

Amount given to cashier: $350

Exact change: _____

10. Prices of items: $21.45; $12.50; $35; $41.65; $1.54

Amount given to cashier: $150

Exact change: _____

Find out how much each customer gave the cashier for each purchase. The first one has been done for you. (Hint: Use a calculator and add the change to the total cost of the items.)

11. Prices of items: $15.67; $23.54; $32

    Amount given to cashier: ____$75____

    Exact change: $3.79

12. Prices of items: $41.65; $11.43; $98.54

    Amount given to cashier: _____

    Exact change: $8.38

13. Prices of items: $9.34; $1.67; $.87; $.24

    Amount given to cashier: _____

    Exact change: $7.88

Apply the Idea

Use the prices of these items to solve exercises 14 to 16.

pen: $5.99   pencils: box of 25 for $3.50

calculator: $12.99   book covers: $.59 each

binder: $4.79   folders: $.49 each

notebooks: $1.79 each

14. George bought two pens, five folders, and two notebooks. He handed the clerk a $20 bill.

    a. About how much will George receive as change?

    _____

    b. Exactly how much will George receive as change?

    _____

15. Juan bought two book covers, one box of pencils, and a notebook. He received $4 back as change. How much did he give to the clerk? _____

16. Suppose you bought three folders, two pens, and a binder. How much would you have to give the clerk in order to receive exactly $2 as change? _____

Write About It

17. Which of the two calculator methods explained in Extend the Idea would you prefer to use to calculate your change? Explain why.

    _____

    _____

    _____

◢6●3 Installment Buying

◢ IN THIS LESSON, YOU WILL LEARN

To find the installment cost for a layaway or an installment purchase

WORDS TO LEARN

Installment plan *a sales method whereby a customer makes repeated payments of equal amounts over a definite time period until the total cost is paid*

Layaway plan *a sales method whereby a store saves an item on which the customer makes a deposit until the customer has paid the total cost over a specific period of time*

Deposit *a partial payment for an item that holds, or reserves, that item for the customer*

Weekly News Report
1-year subscription
$36 off the cover price.
Pay $90 or 4 equal installments of
$23.50 each month for four months.

New Idea

When you buy an item on an **installment plan** (ihn-STAWL-muhnt plan), you make a number of equal payments over a specified period of time. Usually, paying by installments costs the buyer more money. To find the cost for the total purchase, multiply the installment amount by the number of payments.

Example: Calculate the cost of the installments for a 1-year subscription to *Weekly News Report*.

Installment Amount × Number of Installments = Total Price

$$\$23.50 \times 4 = \$94$$

If you buy a year's subscription to this magazine on an installment plan, you pay $94. This is $4 more than if you pay for the subscription in one lump sum.

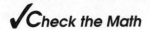

1. Leroy wants to buy a camera he saw advertised in the newspaper. The camera costs $245.95. The ad says that an installment plan of 5 monthly payments of $50 is available. Leroy figures that he could pay for the camera in five installments and save $4.05. Is he correct? Why or why not?

_____

Focus on the Idea

To calculate total cost when buying with installment payments, multiply the amount of each installment by the number of installments.

Practice

Find the total cost for each purchase. The first one has been done for you.

	Amount of each Installment	Number of Installments	Total Cost
2.	$63.50	4	$254.00
3.	$34.00	3	_____
4.	$109.50	5	_____
5.	$180.00	2	_____
6.	$11.50	12	_____
7.	$21.50	4	_____

Extend the Idea

Some stores offer customers a layaway plan for the purchase of some items. A **layaway plan** (LAY-uh-way plan) requires a customer to leave some money toward the cost of an item, which the store then holds until the total cost has been paid over a period of time. A **deposit** (dee-PAHZ-iht) is the specific amount of money paid to hold the item until the total cost has been paid. Once a customer has paid the total cost, the item belongs to the customer. Here is how Martha bought a $160 coat on a layaway plan.

Example: Price of coat: $160
Deposit: 10% of purchase price

Remember

To find the amount needed for a deposit, multiply the price by the percent of deposit.

$160 × 0.10 = $16
Weekly payment: 10% of purchase price, or $16

Martha made a deposit of $16 to start the layaway plan. If she then paid $26 each week for 3 weeks, how much would she still owe toward the price of the coat? To find out, do the following:

Step 1 Subtract to find out how much Martha owes after making the deposit.
$160 − $16 = $144 ← Amount owed after deposit

Step 2 Multiply to find out how much Martha pays in her 3 payments of $26 each.
$26 × 3 = $78

Step 3 Subtract to find out how much Martha still owes.
$144 − $78 = $66 ← Amount still owed

Martha must pay this $66 before she can take the coat home. If she makes two more payments of $26 each, how much will her final payment be?
$26 × 2 = $52 $66 − $52 = $14
Her final payment will be $14.

✓Check Your Understanding

8. Suppose Martha had wanted to make 4 equal weekly payments to pay for the coat after having paid her $16.00 deposit. How much would she pay each week? _____

Practice

Complete the calculations for each item bought on a layaway plan, which calls for a deposit and a number of equal payments. The first one has been done for you.

9. Price of suit: $180

    10% deposit: ___$180 × 0.10 = $18___

    Amount owed after deposit: ___$180 − $18 = $162___

    Amount of each of 3 equal payments: ___$162 ÷ 3 = $54___

    Amount remaining to be paid after first payment:
    ___$162 − $54 = $108___

10. Price of luggage: $360

    10% deposit: _____

    Amount owed after deposit: _____

    Amount of each of 3 equal payments: _____

    Amount remaining to be paid after first payment: _____

11. Price of sneakers: $95

10% deposit: _____

Amount owed after deposit: _____

Amount of each of 3 equal payments: _____

12. Price of 2 pairs of blue jeans: $37.80 each

10% deposit: _____

Amount owed after deposit: _____

Amount of each of 4 equal payments: _____

Apply the Idea

13. Harry purchased a stereo set from Mario's Music Store. The total cost was $475.50. Harry is paying for the set in 6 equal monthly installments. How much does Harry pay each month? _____

14. Nicki has a layaway plan for a $54 pair of jeans and two sweaters that cost $42 each. She makes a 10% deposit and pays the remaining amount in 4 equal payments. How much is each of her four payments? _____

15. Suppose you buy a $240 coat on a layaway plan. You pay a 10% deposit, then 3 more weekly payments of 10% each. How much more do you owe? _____

16. Mrs. Justice bought a one-year subscription to a weekly magazine. The total cost of the subscription is $129. If she pays in 12 equal installments, how much will she pay each month? _____

17. Jena bought 3 sweatshirts and 3 pairs of sweatpants, each at $19.90. She put all the clothes on a layaway plan, making a 15% deposit. If she pays 15% of the price each week for 3 more weeks, how much will she owe? _____

Write About It

18. What is the advantage of buying something on layaway?

_____

_____

19. What is the disadvantage of using a layaway plan?

_____

_____

▶6•4 Using Bank Credit Cards and Charge Accounts

▶**IN THIS LESSON, YOU WILL LEARN**

To determine a monthly credit card bill based on monthly interest charged on the unpaid balance

WORDS TO LEARN

Charge *to buy an item now, then pay for it later*

Credit card account *a credit account issued by a bank that allows a person to charge purchases*

Charge account *a credit account issued by a store that allows a person to charge purchases*

Unpaid balance *the amount owed on a credit card account or store charge account*

Ray charges a $350 VCR on his Bankcard of the U.S. (19.5% annual interest). He pays $50 towards his balance on the first month's bill.

New Idea

Ray is buying an item now and paying for it later. This means that he will **charge** (chahrj) the item he purchases. A **credit card account** (KRED-iht khard uh-KOWNT), an account issued by a bank, allows a person to charge a purchase at many different places. A **charge account** (chahrj uh-KOWNT), an account issued by a store, allows a person to charge a purchase at a store in its chain. Banks and businesses often charge a fee for using credit. This fee is called interest, which is calculated on the **unpaid balance** (uhn-PAYD BAL-uhnz), or amount still owed.

Example: What will be the amount of Ray's bill for the second month?

Step 1 Find the unpaid balance. $350 − $50 = $300

Step 2 Find the monthly interest rate. Divide the annual rate by 12. 19.5% ÷ 12 = 1.625%

Step 3 Find the amount of monthly interest charged on the unpaid balance. $300 × 0.01625 = $4.875 or $4.88

For the second month, Ray's interest will be $4.88. Interest is calculated each month (except the first) on the unpaid balance in the account.

To find the amount of Ray's second month's bill, add the interest charges to the unpaid balance.

$300.00   Unpaid balance
+   4.88   Interest
$304.88   Amount owed

Focus on the Idea

To calculate interest on a credit account, multiply the unpaid balance times the monthly interest rate. Then add the amount of monthly interest to the unpaid balance and any new costs.

Practice

For each annual interest rate, write the monthly rate as a percent and as a decimal. The first one is done for you.

	Annual Interest Rate	Monthly Interest Rate	
		Percent	Decimal
1.	8.75%	0.73%	0.0073
2.	12.6%	_____	_____
3.	26%	_____	_____
4.	14.8%	_____	_____

Find the monthly interest rate and the amount of the second month's bill for each charge account purchase.

	Purchase Price	First Month's Payment	Annual Interest Rate	Monthly Interest Rate	Second Month's Bill
5.	$500	$150	18.6%	_____	_____
6.	$150	$25	22.0%	_____	_____
7.	$1,200	$400	9.6%	_____	_____
8.	$375	$125	20.5%	_____	_____

Apply the Idea

9. Justin bought a $150 CD player, using a credit card that charges 11.5% annual interest beginning with the second month's payment. Justin paid $25 on his first month's bill. What will his next month's bill be? _____

Write About It

10. What are some advantages and disadvantages of using a credit card to make purchases? Use another sheet of paper to write your answer.

⬤6●5 Reviewing Credit Plans

◀ **IN THIS LESSON, YOU WILL LEARN**

To compare costs of installment buying, layaway plans, and credit card purchases

WORDS TO LEARN

Payment plan *a method of paying for items purchased by using either an installment plan, a layaway plan, or a credit card*

Bob decided to buy Lifetimes Magazine using a credit card. His credit card account charges 15.5% annual interest. Bob paid $20 on his first month's bill and the remainder of the unpaid balance when his second month's bill arrived. Compare this method of payment with the other two methods of paying that Bob might have chosen.

> **Order Your One-Year Subscription to**
> # LIFETIMES MAGAZINE
> **right away**
> *Choose one of the three easy methods of paying:*
> • Check ($49.95)
> • 4 monthy installments ($13.50 each, Service charge included)
> • Credit Card ($49.95)

New Idea

When you buy an item under a **payment plan** (PAY-muhnt plan), you use an installment plan, a layaway plan, or a credit card as a method of payment. To compare the cost of paying by check, by credit card, or by installment payments, find each total amount for the one-year subscription.

Check: $49.95   Total Cost

Installments: $13.50 × 4 = $54   Total Cost

Credit Card: $49.95 − $20 = $29.95   Unpaid Balance

15.5% ÷ 12 = 1.29%   Monthly Interest

$29.95 × 0.0129 = $.39   Interest

$20 + $29.95 + $.39 = $50.34   Total Cost

You can see that buying on the installment plan would cost the most. Paying by check would cost the least.

◀ **Focus on the Idea**

To compare different payment plans, find and compare the total cost of a purchase, including interest and service charges, for each plan.

Find the total cost of each plan. The first one is done for you.

1. Purchase price: $159.95
   4 installments of $41.25 each = ___$165.00___ Total cost
   Layaway plan with $5 service charge = ___$164.95___ Total cost

2. Purchase price: $575
   3 installments of $194 each = _____ Total cost
   Layaway plan with $15 service charge = _____ Total cost

3. Purchase price: $269
   5 installments of $55 each = _____ Total cost
   Layaway plan with $4.50 service charge = _____ Total cost

Use the following information for exercises 4 to 6.

Purchase Price	Layaway Service Charge	Four Installment Payments	Total Credit Card Interest
$150	$4.25	$39 each	$3.13
$450	$3	$113.50 each	$2.25
$240	$4	$60.50 each	$4.10

What is the total cost of the purchase using each payment plan?

	Item	Layaway	Installment	Credit card
4.	$150	_____	_____	_____
5.	$450	_____	_____	_____
6.	$240	_____	_____	_____

Apply the Idea

7. Jean charged a $169 camera to her credit card, which charges 18% annual interest. She paid $24 on her first month's bill. The second month she paid the balance. Sally bought the same camera and paid 3 equal installments of $57.75.

   a. How much interest did Jean pay? _____

   b. Who paid more? How much more? _____

Write About It

8. Describe a situation in which you would use a layaway plan, an installment plan, or a credit card. Tell why the credit plan you chose is best to use for that situation.

   _____

   _____

Chapter 6   Review

In This Chapter, You Have Learned

- To calculate the sales tax and the purchase price of an item
- To estimate and calculate the amount of change received
- To find the installment cost for a layaway or an installment purchase
- To determine a monthly credit card bill based on monthly interest charged on the unpaid balance
- To compare costs of installment buying plans, layaway plans, and credit card account purchases

Words You Know

Write the letter of the phrase in Column 2 that defines each word in Column 1.

Column 1	Column 2
1. credit card account _____	**a.** a card, issued by a bank, used to charge items
2. sales tax _____	**b.** an item on which a sales tax is charged
3. Installment plan _____	**c.** the amount owed on a credit card account, store charge-card account, or layaway plan
4. taxable item _____	**d.** a percentage charge added to the price of an item
5. unpaid balance _____	**e.** a method of buying items for which a customer makes repeated payments of equal amounts until the total cost is paid

More Practice

Complete the chart.

	Price	Sales Tax Rate	Amount of Tax	Purchase Price
6.	$250	3%	_____	_____
7.	$12.95	8.75%	_____	_____

Estimate the amount of change for each of the following:

8. Total cost: $46.75   Amount given to cashier: $50

Estimated change: _____

9. Total cost: $11.62   Amount given to cashier: $20

Estimated change: _____

Find the exact change due for each of the following:

10. Cost of items: $12.75; $34.55; $10

    Amount given to cashier: $100

    Exact change: _____

11. Cost of items: $1.79; $2.54; $0.32; $4.55

    Amount given to cashier: $10

    Exact change: _____

Complete each chart.

	Amount of each Installment	Number of Installments	Purchase Price
12.	$113.50	4	_____
13.	$255.00	6	_____
14.	$57.45	4	_____
15.	$28.00	3	_____

	Purchase Price	First Month's Payment	Annual Interest Rate	Monthly Interest Rate	Second Month's Bill
16.	$540	$120	21%	_____	_____
17.	$245	$25	19.5%	_____	_____
18.	$2,400	$150	15.5%	_____	_____

Problems You Can Solve

19. Hank bought 2 sweatshirts at $17.75 each and 3 T-shirts at $12.95 each. He put all the clothes on a layaway plan, paying a 10% deposit. If he pays 10% of the price each week for 3 more weeks, how much more will he owe? _____

20. Cheryl charged a $1,600 lounge chair to her credit card account, which charges 21% annual interest. She paid $150 on her first month's bill. On the second month's bill, she paid the balance. Joel bought the same chair and made 5 equal payments of $330 each.

    a. How much interest did Cheryl pay? _____

    b. Who paid the higher total cost? How much higher?

    _____

21. **For Your Portfolio** Research the kinds of credit card accounts available through local banks and charge accounts available in local stores. Make a class presentation to show the various interest rates and terms for each account.

Find the amount of tax and purchase price for each item purchased.

	Price	Tax Rate	Amount of Tax	Purchase Price
1.	$340	4%	_____	_____
2.	$1.89	6.75%	_____	_____
3.	$13.59	3.5%	_____	_____

Estimate the amount of change for each of the following:

4. Total cost: $86.95   Amount given to cashier: $100

   Estimated change: _____

5. Total cost: $13.22   Amount given to cashier: $50

   Estimated change: _____

Find the exact change due for each of the following:

6. Cost of items: $2.75; $44.25; $19

   Amount given to cashier: $70

   Exact change: _____

7. Cost of items: $1.49; $2.34; $.88; $3.79

   Amount given to cashier: $10

   Exact change: _____

Complete each chart.

	Amount of each Installment	Number of Installments	Purchase Price
8.	$77.00	3	_____
9.	$210.00	6	_____
10.	$98.50	5	_____
11.	$31.75	3	_____

	Purchase Price	First Month's Payment	Annual Interest Rate	Monthly Interest Rate	Second Month's Bill
12.	$620	$80	20%	_____	_____
13.	$145	$30	18.5%	_____	_____
14.	$1,875	$170	14.5%	_____	_____

 15. Steve charged a $1,500 computer. He charged it on his credit card, which has an annual interest rate of 17.5%. The first month Steve paid $100 towards his bill. The second month he paid $400. He paid the remaining total during the third month. What was the total cost of the computer, including interest? _____

Chapter 7
Buying Food

OBJECTIVES:

In this chapter, you will learn

- *To calculate amounts of calories and nutrients*
- *To use ratios to describe and compare unit prices*
- *To determine final cost after coupon discounts have been taken*
- *To use proportions to change recipes*

Below are Amy's shopping list and her cents-off coupons.

Grocery shopping takes time and money. Smart shoppers look for special prices and use discount coupons to save money. Think about Amy's list and the cost of groceries. What are some ways to save money on groceries?

Things to buy:

2 rolls paper towels

half dozen eggs

1/4 lb ham

3 loaves bread

15¢ off
2 Rolls of
Paper Towels

20¢ off
3 Loaves
of Bread

◢7•1 Using Nutrition Labels

◣ IN THIS LESSON, YOU WILL LEARN

To calculate amounts of calories and nutrients

WORDS TO LEARN

Calories *units for measuring the energy-producing value in foods*

Nutrients *the useful parts of food that the body needs for growth*

Most labels on food items provide information on the contents. The information includes the size of a serving and many nutrition facts. To get information about her lunch, Tara read the following labels.

HEALTHY CHICKEN NOODLE SOUP

Nutrition Facts

Serving Size: 1 cup (243 g)
Servings per Container: about 2

Amount Per Serving

Calories: 100
Calories from fat: 10

*Percent Daily Value (DV) are based on a 2,000 calorie diet.

Amount/serving	%DV*
Total Fat 1.5g	**2%**
Saturated 0g	**0%**
Polyunsaturated 0.5g	**0%**
Cholesterol 5mg	**2%**
Sodium 450mg	**19%**
Total Carbohydrates 18g	**6%**
Sugars 3g	
Dietary Fiber 3g	**0%**
Protein 4g	

FAT FREE YUMMY CRACKERS

Nutrition Facts

Serving Size: 5 Crackers (15 g)
Servings per Container: about 28

Amount Per Serving

Calories: 60
Calories from fat: 0

*Percent Daily Value (DV) are based on a 2,000 calorie diet.

Amount/serving	%DV*
Total Fat 0g	**0%**
Cholesterol 0mg	**0%**
Sodium 135mg	**6%**
Total Carbohydrates 12g	**4%**
Sugars 0g	
Dietary Fiber 1g	**2%**
Protein 2g	

New Idea

Calories (KAL-uh-reez) are the units that measure the energy-producing value in food. **Nutrients** (NOO-tree-uhnts) are the useful parts of food that the body needs for growth.

Example: If Tara eats two cups of soup and eight crackers, how many calories has she consumed?

Step 1 Find the number of servings consumed, or eaten.
amount eaten ÷ serving amount = total servings
$$2 \text{ cups} \div 1 \text{ cup} = 2 \text{ servings of soup}$$
$$8 \text{ crackers} \div 5 \text{ crackers} = 1\frac{3}{5} \text{ servings of crackers}$$

Step 2 Find the number of calories consumed for each item.
calories per serving × servings = calories consumed
$$100 \times 2 = 200 \text{ calories from soup}$$
$$60 \times 1\frac{3}{5} = 60 \times \frac{8}{5} = 96 \text{ calories from crackers}$$

Step 3 Add to find the total number of calories consumed.
200 calories from soup + 96 calories from crackers = 296 calories

Tara consumed a total of 296 calories.

◀ Focus on the Idea

To calculate the number of calories, first find the number of servings consumed. Divide the amount consumed by the amount per serving. Then multiply the number of servings by the number of calories per serving. Finally, add the calories consumed for each kind of food.

Practice

Use the food labels for the soup and crackers to find the amount of calories in each of the following. The first one is done for you.

1. $\frac{3}{4}$ cup soup   75
2. 15 crackers   _____
3. $\frac{1}{4}$ cup soup   _____
4. 3 crackers   _____
5. $1\frac{1}{2}$ cups soup   _____
6. 12 crackers   _____

Apply the Idea

7. One cup of pasta has 150 calories. If you eat $2\frac{1}{2}$ cups of pasta, how many calories do you consume? _____

✎ Write About It

8. Use the nutrition labels on your food packages to find out which nutrients make up the main part of your diet. Find out which of your favorite foods are highest in calories, carbohydrates, and proteins.

_____

_____

7•2 Using Unit Pricing to Compare Costs

IN THIS LESSON, YOU WILL LEARN

To use ratios to describe and compare unit prices

WORDS TO LEARN

Better buy *the item that gives you more for less money*

Rate *a price for a given quantity of an item*

Unit price *the cost of one unit of an item*

Ratio *a comparison of two numbers*

Madison Variety Store and Galaxy Stationery Store sell many of the same products. The stores are near each other. A wise shopper can compare the prices at each store to see which store has the better buy.

New Idea

To find the **better buy** (BEHT-uhr by), the product that gives you more for less money, you need to compare prices for the same item. Some stores sell items by stating a **rate** (rayt), or a price for a given quantity of an item. The best way to compare prices is to find the **unit price** (YOON-iht prys), which is the cost of one item or of one unit of the item. To find the unit price, first find the **ratio** (RAY-shoh), or comparison of the total cost to the number of units. Do this by writing a fraction with the cost in the numerator and the quantity of units in the denominator. Then find an equivalent ratio for the unit price.

Example: Write the rate for markers at Madison Variety Store as a ratio. Six markers sell for $2.00. The ratio can be written as $\frac{\$2.00}{6}$ markers.

To find the unit price for the markers at Madison Variety Store, find a ratio equal to $\frac{\$2.00}{6}$ that has a denominator of 1. To do this, divide the numerator and the denominator by 6.

$$\frac{\$2.00}{6} = \frac{(\$2 \div 6)}{(6 \div 6)} = \frac{\$0.33}{1}$$

At Madison Variety Store, the unit price, or the price of one marker, is $.33.

✓ Check Your Understanding

1. If Galaxy Stationery Store sells markers for $.45 each, which store has the better buy? _____

Focus on the Idea

To find the unit price of an item, write the cost and the number of items as a ratio. Then divide the numerator and denominator by the same number so that the denominator equals 1.

Practice

Write each of the following items and prices as a ratio. Then find the unit price for each item. When necessary, round all unit prices to the nearest cent. The first one is done for you.

Items and Prices	Ratio	Unit Price
2. 3 lb of apples for $1.89	$\frac{1.89}{3}$	$.63 per pound
3. 64 oz of detergent for $3.99	_____	_____
4. 5 cans of soup for $4.20	_____	_____
5. 3 boxes of pasta for $2.49	_____	_____
6. 12-oz bag of chips for $1.39	_____	_____

Apply the Idea

7. Joe is buying potato chips for a party. Which is the better buy, 12-ounce bags that cost $2.39 each or 16-ounce bags that cost $2.89 each? Why?

_____

_____

8. Sal's Deli is selling bologna at $1.49 per half pound. Milt's Deli is selling it at $.99 per quarter pound. Which deli is selling bologna for less? How much less?

_____

_____

✎ Write About It

9. Write a paragraph explaining how you can use unit pricing to help you find the better buy when shopping for food.

_____

_____

_____

_____

7•3 Using Coupons

IN THIS LESSON, YOU WILL LEARN

To determine final cost after coupon discounts have been taken

WORDS TO LEARN

Manufacturer's coupon *cents-off coupon that can be used in any store that sells a certain product*

Store coupon *cents-off coupon that can be used only in particular stores*

Vernon has a manufacturer's coupon for Fido Dog Food. He can get a discount on that brand of dog food in any store. A local store sells Fido Dog Food for $.47 per can and a store brand of dog food for $.37 per can. Vernon needs to compare prices to see if he gets a better buy with his coupon.

$.35 off
3 Cans of
Fido Dog Food

New Idea

A **manufacturer's coupon** (man-yoo-FAK-chuhr-uhrz KOO-pahn) is a cents-off coupon that can be used in any store that sells a certain product. A **store coupon** (stawr KOO-pahn) is a cents-off coupon that can be used only in particular stores. To compare the costs of items with and without cents-off coupons, find the unit price of each item, including the coupon discount.

Example: Find the unit price of Fido Dog Food.

Step 1 Find the price with the coupon discount.

3 cans at $.47 each = $1.41

cost with coupon: $1.41 − $.35 = $1.06

Step 2 Use the new cost to find the new unit price.

unit price with coupon = $\frac{\$1.06}{3}$ = about $.35 per can

Vernon decided to buy Fido Dog Food at $.35 per can with the coupon rather than the store brand at $.37 per can.

Focus on the Idea

To compare prices of items with and without cents-off coupons, find the unit prices of the items after subtracting coupon discounts.

Practice

Find the price of the following items with the coupon discount. The first one is done for you.

	Item	Coupon Discount	Cost with Coupon
1.	Starwars Tuna 6-oz can $1.39	30 cents off 2 cans	2 cans $2.48
2.	Lovely Face Soap 3 bars $2.09	45 cents off 3 bars	3 bars of soap _____
3.	1 dozen eggs $1.19	50 cents off 3 dozen	3 dozen eggs _____
4.	5 lb of loose potatoes $2.75	20 cents off per lb	5 lb of potatoes _____
5.	Home-Made Soup $.89 per can	75 cents off 2 cans	2 cans of soup _____

Apply the Idea

Use the following product information to solve exercise 6.

$.25 off 3 bars Handbar Soap

$.35 off 2 cans Great-Dog Dog Food

$.30 off 1 quart Cow's Best Milk

Handbar Soap: $.55 per bar   Gentle Soap: $.50 per bar
Great-Dog Dog Food: $.37 per can   Variety Dog Food: $.45 a can
Store Brand Milk: $.99 per qt   Cow's Best Milk: $1.25 per qt

6. Determine the better buy for each item on the following shopping list. You can use any cents-off coupons shown above and buy any brand. Then calculate your total bill.

		Brand	Cost with Coupon
a.	2 cans dog food	_____	_____
b.	3 bars soap	_____	_____
c.	$\frac{1}{2}$ gallon (2 quarts) milk	_____	_____
d.	total bill:	_____	_____

Write About It

7. Name some advantages and disadvantages of using "Buy one, get one free" coupons.

_____

_____

How can this recipe be changed to serve more people?

MEAT LOAF (Serves 4)
Ingredients:
- 1 lb ground beef   • 1 tsp salt
- 1 can condensed   • 1/8 tsp pepper
  mushroom soup
- 1 egg   • 1/2 cup bread
                         crumbs
- 1/4 cup chopped onion

New Idea

A **recipe** (REHS-uh-pee) gives instructions for making a food dish. It includes the **ingredients** (ihn-GREE-dee-uhnts), or food items, that are needed to make the dish, and the number of people served.

A **proportion** (proh-PAWR-shuhn) is a statement that two ratios are equal. Use a proportion to find the way to change a recipe.

Example: Find the amount of ground beef needed to make the meat loaf recipe for 6 people.

Step 1 Write a proportion comparing ingredients and number of people.

Use the variable x to represent the unknown amount of ground beef for the new number of people.

$$\frac{\text{amount of ingredient}}{\text{number of people}} \quad \rightarrow \quad \frac{1 \text{ lb}}{4 \text{ people}} = \frac{x \text{ lb}}{6 \text{ people}}$$

Step 2 Solve the proportion for the variable x.

$\frac{1}{4} = \frac{x}{6}$

$4x = 6 \cdot 1$ ← Cross multiply.

$\frac{4x}{4} = \frac{6}{4}$ ← Divide both sides by 4.

$x = 1\frac{1}{2}$ ← Simplify.

You will need $1\frac{1}{2}$ pounds of ground beef to make enough meat loaf for 6 people.

Focus on the Idea

Use proportions to change a recipe. To solve a proportion, first cross multiply. Then solve for the unknown number.

Practice

Adjust the amount of each ingredient you would use to serve the new number of people. The first one is done for you.

	Number of People	Amount of Ingredient	New Number of People	Adjusted Amount of Ingredient
1.	3	4 cups	6	*8 cups*
2.	3	4 cups	4	_____
3.	3	4 cups	2	_____
4.	3	4 cups	20	_____
5.	3	$1\frac{1}{2}$ cups	5	_____
6.	3	$1\frac{1}{2}$ cups	1	_____

Apply the Idea

7. How much soup, eggs, and bread crumbs will you need to make meat loaf for 6 people, using the recipe on page 124?

_____

8. A recipe for 1 pound of chicken salad calls for $1\frac{1}{2}$ cups of diced chicken and $\frac{1}{2}$ cup of mayonnaise. If 1 pound of chicken salad will serve 4 people, how much chicken and mayonnaise will you need to serve chicken salad to 10 people?

_____

9. A recipe for salad dressing calls for $\frac{1}{4}$ cup of olive oil, $\frac{1}{2}$ teaspoon of lemon juice, and $1\frac{1}{2}$ teaspoons of anchovy paste. Chef Charles is making one half of this recipe. He uses $\frac{1}{4}$ cup of olive oil, $\frac{1}{4}$ teaspoon of lemon juice, and $\frac{1}{4}$ teaspoon of anchovy paste. Are these amounts correct? Why or why not?

_____

✏ Write About It

10. Bring your favorite recipe to class. Double it. Then cut it in half. Explain what steps you took to change the recipe.

_____

_____

Chapter 7   Review

In This Chapter, You Have Learned

- To calculate amounts of calories and nutrients
- To use ratios to describe and compare unit prices
- To determine final cost, using coupon discounts
- To use proportions to change recipes

Words You Know

From the lists of "Words to Learn," choose the word or phrase that best completes each statement.

1. You can use a(n) _____ in any store to receive cents off the price of a certain product the store sells.

2. The useful parts of food the body needs for growth are known as _____.

3. To make a food dish for a certain number of people, you need to find the correct amount of each _____ that is listed in the recipe.

4. To compare the cost of two products, use the _____ to determine how much one item of each product costs.

5. A(n) _____ is a list of food items needed and the cooking instructions for preparing a particular dish.

6. A(n) _____ is the unit used to measure the energy-producing value in food.

7. When you compare two of the same kind of item to determine which one gives you more product for less money, you are seeking the _____.

More Practice

In 2 ounces of tuna there are 70 calories. Find the number of calories for each amount of tuna.

8. 6 oz _____   9. 1 oz _____

Find the cost of each item, using the coupon discount.

Item	Coupon Discount	Cost with Coupon
10. hot cocoa mix $2.39 a can	45 cents off 2 cans	2 cans: _____
11. skin care soap 4 bars: $2.19	75 cents off 4 bars	4 bars: _____
12. crackers 1 box: $1.39	50 cents off 3 boxes	3 boxes: _____

Find the unit price for each of the following items. (Round all answers to the nearest cent.)

13. 3 cans of dog food for $1.19; unit price: _____ per can

14. 5 lb of potatoes for $2.29; unit price: _____ per lb

15. 1 lb of chips for $1.88 (16 oz = 1 lb);
unit price: _____ per oz

Find the cost of each of the following items.

Item	Price	Amount Bought	Cost
16. grapes	$2.45/lb	5 lb	_____
17. soup	$1.89/can	8 cans	_____
18. tissue	$2.25/box	3 boxes	_____

Problems You Can Solve

19. To make 1 cup of hot cocoa, you add 6.5 ounces of hot water to 1.5 ounces of cocoa mix. How many ounces of water would you need to make 6 cups of hot cocoa? _____

20. When Rita makes her salsa dressing, she uses $2\frac{1}{2}$ teaspoons of hot pepper for every 16 ounces of dressing. If she makes only 8 ounces of dressing, how much hot pepper will she use?

_____

21. The directions on a can of coffee say to use $1\frac{1}{4}$ scoops of coffee for every 6 ounces of water. Bill fills his coffee machine with 32 ounces of water. How many scoops of coffee should he use? _____

22. Landmark Brand ground beef is priced at $1.99 per pound. Russ has a coupon for Landmark beef worth $.80 off the cost of 3 pounds. The store brand of ground beef costs $1.69 per pound. Russ needs to buy 3 pounds. Which is the better buy, Landmark or the store brand? Why?

_____

23. **For Your Portfolio**   Look back at Amy's grocery list on page 117. Work with a partner to find the cost of Amy's groceries in a market near you. Then compare the prices with those of another store in your neighborhood. Assume you can use her coupons. Write about your findings and determine which store has the better buy on each item.

_____

_____

_____

Chapter 7   Practice Test

The label on a package of cookies says that 6 cookies have 330 calories. Use this information to complete exercises 1 and 2. (Round answers to the nearest tenth.)

        10 cookies   2 cookies

1. calories: _____   2. calories: _____

Find the cost of each item, using the coupon discount.

Item	Coupon Discount	Cost with Coupon
3. 1 box of herbal tea bags, $2.79	75 cents off 2 boxes	2 boxes: _____
4. 4 heads of lettuce, $.99 a head	buy 1, get 1 free	4 heads: _____

Find the unit price for each of the following items. (Round answers to the nearest cent.)

5. 3 cans of corn for $1.69; unit price: _____ per can

6. 2 gallons of milk for $6.89 (4 quarts to a gallon); unit price: _____ per quart

Find the cost of each of the following.

Item	Unit Price	Amount Bought	Cost
7. noodles	$2.05	5 boxes	_____
8. bananas	$0.89	$5\frac{1}{2}$ lb	_____

Solve.

9. To make a quart of lemonade, you add 4 scoops of mix to 32 ounces of water. How many scoops of mix would you need to make one 8-ounce glass of lemonade? _____

10. Mel is making a party mix of cheese crackers, pretzels, and cheese crisps. At the last party, he made enough mix for 10 people by using $\frac{1}{2}$ pound of crackers, $\frac{3}{4}$ pound of pretzels, and $1\frac{1}{2}$ pounds of crisps. This time, there will be 25 people at the party. How much of each item should he use for his party mix?

_____

Chapter 8

Transportation

OBJECTIVES:

In this chapter, you will learn

- *To use train and bus schedules*
- *To compare various commuting costs*
- *To calculate the total purchase price of an automobile*
- *To calculate costs of automobile insurance and maintenance*

Julie got a new job working 5 days per week. She can travel to work by train, bus, or car. The chart shows the cost for each method of transportation.

	Fare	Gasoline per day	Tolls and Parking per day
Train	$5.75 round trip each day	—	—
Bus	$31.25 round trip each week	—	—
Car	—	$2.50	$7.80

Which way of traveling will cost Julie the least? How much will it cost her each week to travel this way? You will be able to answer these questions when you complete Chapter 8.

▶8•1 Using Public Transportation

Patty lives in Belmar, New Jersey. She needs to arrive at work in New York City by 9:00 A.M. It is a 15-minute walk from the bus station to her office. Which bus should she take?

Belmar/New York City Bus Schedule			
Bel. to N.Y.C		N.Y.C. to Bel.	
Leave Bel.	Arrive N.Y.C.	Leave N.Y.C.	Arrive Bel.
6:01 A.M.	7:52 A.M.	4:30 P.M.	6:24 P.M.
6: 30 A.M.	8:13 A.M.	4:50 P.M.	6:32 P.M.
7:01 A.M.	8:55 A.M.	5:01 P.M.	6:57 P.M.
7:15 A.M.	9:10 A.M.	5:20 P.M.	7:15 P.M.

New Idea

A bus or train **schedule** (SKEH-jool) shows when buses or trains leave and arrive at specific places. You can use a schedule to plan the best **departure time** (dee-PAHR-chuhr tyem), or time to leave, to get to work on time. A schedule helps you predict your **arrival time** (uh-RY-vuhl tyem), or time to get to a specific place.

Example: Determine which bus Patty should take to work.

Patty must arrive in N.Y.C. by 8:45, since she has a 15-minute walk to work. Only the 6:01 bus and the 6:30 bus will get Patty to work on time.

◀ Focus on the Idea

When you are traveling on a bus or a train, refer to a schedule to get where you are going on time.

Practice

Use the Belmar/New York City bus schedule for exercises 1 to 3. The first one is done for you.

1. Patty leaves work at 5:00 P.M. What is the first bus she can catch to Belmar? What is its arrival time in Belmar?
   <u>5:20 P.M.; 7:15 P.M.</u>

2. If you lived in Belmar and wanted to arrive in N.Y.C. by 9:00 A.M., what is the departure time of the latest bus you could take from Belmar? _____

3. Darryl arrives at the N.Y.C. bus station at 4:35 P.M. How long must he wait for the next bus to Belmar? What will be his arrival time in Belmar? _____

Apply the Idea

Use this train schedule to solve exercises 4 to 6.

INBOUND Train Departure Times							
Manasquan	5:14	6:10	7:10		9:14		11:14
Spring Lake	5:18	6:10	7:10		9:18		11:18
Long Branch	5:50	6:50	7:50	8:50	9:50	10:50	11:50
Allenhurst	5:33	6:33	7:33		9:33		11:33

4. Cheryl lives in Spring Lake and works in Long Branch. Her office is a 5-minute walk from the Long Branch train station. She must start work at 7:45 A.M. What is the latest train she can take to arrive to work on time? _____

5. Chris lives in Spring Lake and works in Allenhurst. She leaves her house at 6:50 A.M. and walks for 10 minutes to the train station. When will Chris arrive in Allenhurst? _____

6. Mark works in Manasquan. He has a business meeting at 12:15 P.M. in Allenhurst. It takes 15 minutes to get from the Allenhurst train station to the meeting place by taxi. If Mark takes the 11:14 train from Manasquan, about how early will he be for his appointment? _____

Write About It

7. Describe your commute to school. Include the walk to the bus or train. Time the various parts of your trip from the time you leave home to the time you reach school. State what time you should leave home and what time you must be in school in order to be on time for your first class.

_____

_____

8•2 Calculating Commuting Costs

IN THIS LESSON, YOU WILL LEARN
To compare various commuting costs

WORDS TO LEARN
Commuting *traveling to and from work or school on a regular basis*

Commuter *a person who travels to and from work or school*

Destination *the place where you want to be when you complete your trip*

Round-trip *a trip to a place and back, usually over the same route*

Hector starts his new job next week. He must decide whether to take the train or the bus. A book of 20 round-trip train tickets costs $225, but the train would leave Hector 12 blocks from his job. A local bus could take him between work and the train station for $1.25 each way. A book of 10 round-trip tickets for a commuter bus costs $120. The bus would leave Hector 2 blocks from his job, so he could walk the rest of the way to work.

New Idea

Commuting (kuh-MYOOT-ihng) is traveling to and from work or school on a regular basis. A person commuting to and from work or school is a **commuter** (kuh-MYOOT-uhr).

The place where you want to be when you complete your trip is your **destination** (dehs-tuh-NAY-shuhn). A trip to your destination and back again, usually over the same route, is called a **round-trip** (ROWND-trihp).

Example: Determine whether Hector should take the train and local bus or the commuter bus to work and back if he wants to spend the least amount of money possible.

To find which method of commuting would cost Hector the least, compare the total cost of one round-trip by train and local bus to the cost of one round-trip by commuter bus.

Step 1   Find the daily cost for commuting by train. To do this, divide the total cost of the book of tickets by the number of round-trip tickets it contains.

$225 total cost ÷ 20 round-trip tickets = $11.25 per round-trip ticket

Step 2   Find the daily cost of taking the local bus. This is $1.25 twice a day (from the train to work, then from work to the train).

$1.25 × 2 = $2.50 each day for bus fare

Step 3   Add to find the daily cost.

$11.25   ← Train ticket

+ 2.50   ← Bus Ticket

$13.75   ← Cost per round-trip by train and bus

Step 4   Find the daily cost by commuter bus. To do this, divide the cost of the bus-ticket book by the number of round-trips.

$120 ÷ 10 = $12 per round-trip by commuter bus

Step 5   Compare the costs of the two methods. Subtract the daily cost of the commuter bus from the daily cost of the train and local bus.

$13.75 − $12 = $1.75

Hector should take the commuter bus because it would cost $1.75 less each day than taking the train and local bus.

✓Check the Math

1. Hector decided that if he takes the train, he could walk the 12 blocks between the train station and his destination rather than take a local bus. If he does this, he believes that the book of train tickets is the better buy. Is he correct? Why or why not?

_____

_____

◤Focus on the Idea

To compare commuting costs, find and compare the total daily cost for one round-trip for each method of transportation. Be sure to include all costs.

Practice

Complete the chart. Round answers to the nearest cent. The first one is done for you.

Method of Transportation	Cost of Ticket Book	Round-trip Tickets in Book	Daily Cost
2. Train A	$175	22	$175 ÷ 22 = $7.95
3. Bus A	$125	20	_____
4. Train B	$75	5	_____
5. Bus B	$35	3	_____

Use the chart above for exercises 6 and 7.

6. Which bus-ticket book, A or B, is the better buy?

_____

7. Which train-ticket book, A or B, is the better buy?

_____

Extend the Idea

Hector is considering driving his car to work instead of taking a train or a bus. This would be 30-miles round-trip. Hector can drive 16 miles on each gallon of gasoline. To calculate the cost of driving, he must consider the costs of gasoline, parking fees, and tolls.

Example: Gasoline costs $1.24 per gallon. Parking costs $6.75 per day. Tolls will cost $1.50 per day. How much will it cost Hector each day to drive to work?

To determine the cost of gasoline per day, first find the number of gallons of gasoline used each day.

$\dfrac{30 \text{ miles}}{16}$ ← miles to and from work
← miles per gallon

↓

1.875 ← gallons per day

Then multiply the cost per gallon times the number of gallons. Round your answer to the nearest cent.

$1.24 per gallon × 1.875 gallons per day = $2.33 per day for gasoline

Add all of Hector's daily driving costs.

$\begin{array}{ll} \$\ 6.75 & \leftarrow \text{parking} \\ 1.50 & \leftarrow \text{tolls} \\ \underline{+\ 2.33} & \leftarrow \text{gasoline} \\ \$10.58 & \leftarrow \text{total} \end{array}$

It will cost Hector $10.58 each day to drive to work.

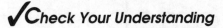
8. If Hector drives to and from work 5 days per week, how much would he spend on gasoline? _____

Practice

Find the total cost of gasoline. Round to the nearest hundreth or nearest cent, when necessary. The first one is done for you.

	Number of Miles	Miles per Gallon	Cost per Gallon of Gasoline	Total Cost of Gasoline
9.	50	18	$1.17	50 ÷ 18 = 2.78; 2.78 × $1.17 = $3.25
10.	125	22	$1.29	_____
11.	75	14.5	$1.14	_____

Apply the Idea

 12. Sam must decide whether to take the train or drive his car to work. The store where he works is 25 miles from his house. Sam's car gets 19 miles to a gallon of gasoline. He pays $1.20 per gallon of gasoline. A book of 34 round-trip train tickets costs $175. Which method of transportation will cost less per day? How much less per day?

_____

13. Pam lives 45 miles from her office and drives to work. She must pay a bridge toll of $1.75 going to and coming from work. Her car gets 21 miles to a gallon of gasoline. If Pam pays $1.22 per gallon, how much does she spend each day on round-trip transportation to her job? _____

14. Doug and Jean work different shifts at the same office. Doug takes the bus to work. He pays $72.50 for a book of 20 round-trip bus tickets. Jean takes the train. She pays $170.50 for a book of 55 round-trip train tickets. Who is paying more in commuter costs? How much more is that per day?

_____

✎ Write About It

15. Trains and buses are types of public transportation. Driving your own car is private transportation. What are some advantages of using public transportation? What are some advantages of using private transportation?

_____

_____

◄8•3 Buying an Automobile

Ted wants to buy a car that costs $10,050. He has $2,000 to give the dealer as a down payment. Because buying a new car is a major expense, Ted should consider all the alternatives before deciding how to pay. One car dealer offers two different plans.

Plan A   Subtract the down payment from the purchase price. Then charge 2.9% annual interest for one year on the remaining amount owed.

Plan B   Subtract the sum of the down payment and a $750 rebate from the purchase price. Then charge 12.5% annual interest per year on the remaining amount owed.

New Idea

To find the total cost of an automobile, subtract any rebate from the price of the car and add any interest. A **rebate** (REE-bayt) is money given back to the customer by the manufacturer. The rebate may also be subtracted. If you need to borrow money from a bank to pay the remaining amount, you will need to pay interest. **Interest** (INT-trihst) is the fee charged on the remaining amount owed. To calculate interest costs, subtract the **down payment** (down PAY-muhnt), which is the amount of money the customer pays toward the purchase price, from the purchase price. The total cost of the car is the sum of the purchase price and the interest on the loan.

Example: How much will the car cost Ted on Plan A? On Plan B?

To find the cost on *Plan A*:

Step 1   Find the amount of money Ted must borrow. Subtract the down payment from the purchase price.

Purchase Price	−	Down Payment	=	Amount to Be Borrowed
$10,050	−	$2,000	=	$8,050

Step 2   Find the amount of interest Ted will pay on the amount borrowed.

Amount Borrowed	×	Interest Rate	×	Time in Years	=	Amount of Interest
$8,050	×	2.9%	×	1	=	$233.45

Step 3   Add the interest to the purchase price.

Purchase Price	+	Amount of Interest	=	Total Cost
$10,050	+	$233.45	=	$10,283.45

On Plan A, the car will cost Ted $10,283.45.

To find the cost on *Plan B*:

Step 1   To find the amount of money Ted must borrow, add the down payment and rebate. Then subtract that sum from the purchase price.

Down Payment	+	Rebate	=	Total Amount to be Subtracted
$2,000	+	$750	=	$2,750

Purchase Price	−	Down Payment and Rebate	=	Amount to Be Borrowed
$10,050	−	$2,750	=	$7,300

Step 2   Find the amount of interest Ted will pay.

$7,300 × 12.5% × 1 = $912.50 Interest

Step 3   Add the interest to the price after the rebate has been subtracted.

$10,050 − $750 + $912.50 = $10,212.50 Total Cost

On Plan B, the car will cost Ted $10,212.50.

If Ted is sure that he can pay for the car within one year, Plan B, with the rebate option, is the better choice.

✓Check the Math

1. Ted found out that the rebate is not given until after he has borrowed money and purchased the car. He decided that this will not change the total cost. Is he correct? Explain.

_____

_____

Focus on the Idea

Calculate the total cost of a car by adding the interest you will pay on any amount you must borrow to the price of the car. Then subtract the amount of any rebate from the price of the car.

Practice

Complete the chart. The first one is done for you. (Note: In each case, the rebate is given at the beginning of the purchase and is added to the down payment.)

	Purchase Price of Car	Down Payment	Rebate	Annual Rate of Interest	Time	Total Cost of Car
2.	$12,000	$1,000	none	10.5%	1 year	$13,155
3.	$15,700	$1,500	$1,200	12.5%	1 year	_____
4.	$9,775	$800	none	6.6%	1 year	_____
5.	$20,450	$2,500	$1,500	11.5%	1 year	_____

Extend the Idea

You may borrow money to buy a car and take more than one year to pay off the loan. The chart below shows monthly payments on a loan of $10,000 at various interest rates for 2-year and 3-year loans.

Annual Rate of Interest	2-Year Loan Monthly Payments	3-Year Loan Monthly Payments
11%	$466.08	$327.39
12.5%	473.08	334.54
13.25%	476.60	338.15
14%	480.13	341.78

✓Check Your Understanding

6. If you borrow $10,000 for 3 years at an interest rate of 14%, what is the total amount you will pay? Explain your answer.

_____

Practice

Use the chart above to answer exercises 7 to 10. The first one is done for you.

7. How much interest would you pay on a 2-year, $10,000 loan at 11% interest?

   $466.08 × 24 months = $11,185.92; $11,185.92 − $10,000 = $1,185.92

8. What is the total amount you would pay on a 3-year, $10,000 loan at 13.25% interest?

_____

9. How much more interest would you pay on a 3-year, $10,000 loan at 11% interest than on a 2-year loan at the same rate?

_____

10. How much more interest would you pay on a 3-year, $10,000 loan at 14% interest than on the same loan at 11% interest?

_____

Apply the Idea

11. Nancy is buying a car with a purchase price of $11,500. She also is paying extra for two options: air conditioning at $600 and automatic transmission at $1,200. Nancy made a down payment of $1,200. She took a 2-year loan for the remaining amount. Her monthly payments will be $566 per month.

    a. What will be the total cost of the car by the time Nancy pays off her loan? _____

    b. How much of this total cost is interest? What is the purchase price of the car? _____

12. Maria wants to buy a car with a purchase price of $9,900. She wants air conditioning, which will cost her $500 more. The car manufacturer will send her a $250 rebate three months after purchase of the car. Maria has $700 for a down payment, and she will borrow the remainder for 1 year at 13% annual interest.

    a. How much would Maria pay for the car if she did not have to borrow money? _____

    b. What will be Maria's total cost for this car after she has paid back her loan? _____

✎ Write About It

13. Imagine that you are buying a car. Would you prefer to use a rebate as part of a down payment or to receive a rebate three months after you have purchased the car? Explain.

_____

_____

_____

▼8•4 Insuring and Maintaining a Car

▼ **IN THIS LESSON, YOU WILL LEARN**

To calculate costs of automobile insurance and maintenance

WORDS TO LEARN

Car insurance *an agreement in which an insurance company promises to pay your expenses in case of a car accident or theft*

Collision insurance *insurance that covers damage to your car*

Comprehensive insurance *insurance that covers damage to your car when the car is unoccupied*

Deductible *the amount a person must pay before the insurance company begins to pay*

Liability insurance *insurance that pays for bodily injury and property damage for other people if you are responsible for an accident*

Uninsured motorist insurance *insurance that pays for damages caused by an uninsured driver*

Premium *your cost for insurance for a given period of time*

Claim *a request you make of your insurance company telling about an accident or theft and asking them to pay for it*

Alex was in a car accident that caused $1,200 damage to his car. How much will his insurance pay to fix his car? How much does Alex pay each year for car insurance? In this lesson, you will learn to find answers to these and other insurance questions.

Alex's Car Insurance Policy	
Coverages	**Premium**
Bodily Injury & Property Damage Liability	$203.00
Basic Personal Injury with $250 deductible	95.00
Uninsured Motorist with $500 deductible	54.00
Collision with $500 deductible	175.00
Comprehensive with $500 deductible	89.00
Total 6-month premium	$616.00

New Idea

A **car insurance** (kahr ihn-SHOOR-uhns) policy pays for injuries or property damage if there is an accident. **Collision insurance** (kuh-LIZH-un ihn-SHOOR-uhns) covers damage to a car from an accident. Damage to a car from such events as a flood or a fire is covered by **comprehensive insurance** (kahm-pree-HEHN-sihv ihn-SHOOR-uhns).

Most insurance policies have a **deductible** (dee-DUKT-uh-buhl), which is an amount to be paid before the insurance company begins to pay. (Note: If there is no deductible listed on the policy, the insurance pays the entire cost of repair or injury, up to the amount insured.) **Liability insurance** (ly-uh-BIHL-uh-tee ihn-SHOOR-uhns) covers bodily injury and property damage for other people if you are responsible for an accident. Basic personal injury insurance covers the costs of any injuries to oneself. Insurance against **uninsured motorists** (un-ihn-SHOORD MOHT-uhr-ihsts) pays for bodily injury damages caused by any driver who does not have insurance if the costs go beyond basic coverage.

The amount you pay for car insurance is your **premium** (PREE-mee-uhm). To ask the insurance company to pay for any damage, you need to file a **claim** (klaym).

Examples: How much will the insurance company pay Alex on his claim?

$1,200 ← cost of fixing his car

− 500 ← deductible for collision

$ 700 ← paid by the insurance company

How much does Alex pay for car insurance for a year?

Since Alex's premium is for 6 months, multiply the amount of the premium by 2.

$616 × 2 = $1,232 ← premium for 1 year

✓Check the Math

1. Alex said that if he had a $250 deductible for collision, his insurance company would have paid $750 for the repairs. Is he correct? Why or why not?

_____

_____

_____

◤Focus on the Idea

To calculate the annual cost of car insurance, add the premiums for each type of coverage. If the coverage is for six months, multiply the total by 2 to find the cost of the premiums for one year. To calculate the amount an insurance company will pay for repairs or injuries, subtract any deductible from the cost.

Practice

Use Alex's insurance policy to complete the chart. The first one is done for you.

	Injury or Damage	Insurance Pays	Part of Policy that Covers Damage
2.	Repairs of $1,000 to the car that Alex hit	1,000	Bodily Injury & Property Damage Liability
3.	Alex's doctor's bill of $540		
4.	Window repairs of $100 caused by a thrown rock		
5.	$750 damage to Alex's car caused by an uninsured driver		

Extend the Idea

A car owner will want to keep his or her car running smoothly. This requires regular maintenance costs for gasoline and for oil changes.

To calculate the monthly cost for gasoline, divide the average number of miles driven per month by the number of miles per gallon. Then multiply the result by the cost per gallon.

Examples: Alex drives about 1,500 miles each month. His car can go 24 miles on each gallon of gasoline. He pays $1.17 per gallon. How much does Alex spend for gasoline per month?

> 1,500 miles ÷ 24 miles per gallon = 62.5 gallons
> 62.5 gallons × $1.17 = $73.13

Alex pays $73.13 per month for gasoline.

To calculate the cost for oil changes, first determine how often they need to be made.

> Alex has his oil changed every 3,000 miles. He pays $29.95 for this service. Estimate how much Alex spends for oil per month.

> 3,000 miles ÷ 1,500 miles per month = 2 months
> $29.95 ÷ 2 is about $15 per month.

> Alex spends about $15 per month for oil.

✓Check Your Understanding

6. What is Alex's total monthly cost for insurance and maintenance? Explain how you arrived at your answer.

Practice

Complete the chart. The first one is done for you.

	Monthly Gasoline Cost	Monthly Oil Cost	Annual Insurance Premium	Annual Insurance & Maintenance	Monthly Insurance & Maintenance
7.	$150	$8	$1,200	$3,096	$258
8.	$240	$12	$1,450	_____	_____
9.	$75	$5	$975	_____	_____
10.	$450	$7.50	$1,500	_____	_____

Apply the Idea

Use the following insurance coverages and premiums from Charles's 6-month car insurance policy to answer exercises 11 to 14.

Coverage	Premium
Bodily Injury & Property Damage Liability	$223
Basic Personal Injury with $250 deductible	85
Uninsured Motorist with $500 deductible	61
Collision with $250 deductible	245
Comprehensive with $500 deductible	95
Total 6-Month Premium	$709

11. Charles had a car accident. The repair bill was $500. His doctor's bill was $300. How much did Charles pay?

   _____

12. Charles's car, valued at $4,800, was destroyed by a fire. How much should his insurance company pay him for the car? _____

13. Charles drives an average of 1,500 miles each month. His car gets 8 miles to a gallon of gasoline. Gasoline costs $1.24 per gallon. He pays $24 every 2 months to have his oil changed. What is Charles's total monthly cost for insurance and car maintenance? _____

Write About It

14. Why would an insurance company lower the premium when your coverage changes from a $250 to a $500 deductible?

_____

_____

Chapter 8   Review

In This Chapter, You Have Learned
- To use train and bus schedules
- To compare commuting costs
- To calculate the total purchase price of a car and costs of car insurance and maintenance

Words You Know

Write the letter of the phrase in column 2 that best defines each word in column 1.

Column 1	Column 2
1. commuter _____	a. your cost for insurance
2. rebate _____	b. amount subtracted from the claim made to an insurance company
3. deductible _____	
4. premium _____	c. a person who travels to and from work or school
	d. money given back to the customer by a manufacturer

More Practice

5. Buses leave Morganville at 8:03 A.M., 8:12 A.M., 8:30 A.M., and 8:41 A.M. It is a half-hour ride to the Center City bus stop.

    a. If you have to arrive at Center City by 8:45, what is the latest bus you can take? _____

    b. If you have a 15-minute walk to work from the Center City bus stop, and you take the 8:03 bus, what time will you get to work? _____

Complete the chart.

	Transportation Method	Ticket Book Cost	Round-trip Tickets in Book	Daily Cost
6.	Train	$155	30	_____
7.	Bus	$78	12	_____

Complete the chart.

	Miles Driven	Miles per Gallon of Gas	Cost per Gallon of Gas	Total Cost of Gas
8.	116.25	15.5	$1.27	_____
9.	45	19	$1.09	_____

Complete the chart.

	Purchase Price	Down Payment	Rebate	Annual Rate of Interest	Loan Term	Total Cost of Car
10.	$13,500	$2,000	none	11.5%	1 year	_____

Complete the chart.

	Monthly Gasoline Cost	Monthly Oil Cost	Annual Insurance Premium	Annual Insurance & Maintenance	Monthly Insurance & Maintenance
11.	$180	$8.50	$1,100	_____	_____

Problems You Can Solve

12. Erin will borrow $9,000 to buy a new car. She will have to pay $289.35 each month for 3 years. How much will she have paid at the end of the three years? _____

13. Bryan had a car accident. The repair bill for his car was $480. His doctor's bill was $890. His insurance coverages and premiums are:

Coverages	Premium
Bodily Injury & Property Damage Liability	$212
Basic Personal Injury with $500 deductible	65
Uninsured Motorist with $500 deductible	57
Collision with $500 deductible	187
Comprehensive with $250 deductible	150
Total 6-Month Premium	$671

   a. How much did Bryan pay for these bills? _____

   b. How much did his insurance company pay? _____

14. Beverly drives an average of 675 miles each month. Her car gets 19.5 miles to a gallon of gasoline, which costs $1.11. She pays $22 every 4 months to have her oil changed. Her insurance premium is $840 per year. What is Beverly's average monthly cost for gas, insurance, and car maintenance?

_____

15. **For Your Portfolio** Work with a partner. Choose a nearby a town or city in which you might get a job. Research various methods of commuting. Write a report explaining which method of transportation you would use and why.

_____

_____

_____

Chapter 8   Practice Test

1. Trains leave Harrisville at 7:13 A.M., 7:25 A.M., 7:40 A.M., and 7:55 A.M. It is a 45-minute ride to the Valley City train station.

   a. If you have to arrive at Valley City by 8:00 A.M., what is the latest train you can take? _____

   b. If you have a 10-minute walk to work from the train station, and you take the 7:25 train, what time will you get to work? _____

Complete the charts for exercises 2 to 7.

	Miles Driven	Miles per Gallon of Gas	Cost per Gallon of Gas	Total Cost of Gas
2.	205	18.5	$1.07	_____
3.	138.5	9	$1.29	_____

	Purchase Price of Car	Down Payment	Rebate	Annual Rate of Interest	Loan Term Payment	Total Cost of Car
4.	$14,800	$1,000	none	14.5%	1 year	_____
5.	$10,700	$700	*$500	13%	1 year	_____

(*Assume the rebate is given after the car is purchased.)

	Monthly Gasoline Cost	Monthly Oil Cost	Annual Insurance Premium	Annual Insurance & Maintenance	Monthly Insurance & Maintenance
6.	$275	$6.50	$950	_____	_____
7.	$84	$4.23	$1,250	_____	_____

Solve.

8. You borrow $11,000. If you pay $280.39 each month for 4 years, how much did the loan cost? _____

9. A 3-year loan of $9,000 at a rate of 14% has monthly payments of $307.60. The same loan for 5 years has monthly payments of $209.42. How much more do you pay if you borrow the $9,000 over 5 years? _____

10. Carla was hit by an uninsured motorist. Her coverage is:

Coverage	Premiums
Bodily Injury & Property Damage Liability	$280
Basic Personal Injury with $500 deductible	78
Uninsured Motorist with $250 deductible	87
Collision with $750 deductible	165
Total 6-Month Premium	$610

The repair bill for Carla's car was $750. The doctor's bill was $890. How much did Carla have to pay? _____

Chapter 9

Housing

⬛ **OBJECTIVES:**

In this chapter, you will learn

- *To compare housing costs and choose affordable housing*
- *To estimate monthly utility bills*
- *To calculate apartment expenses based on a lease*
- *To calculate amounts of paint and carpet and the costs of painting and carpeting*
- *To calculate the monthly expenses of owning a residence*

The amount of money a family can afford to pay for housing depends on the family's income. Each of the families listed below pays a different amount for housing each month, but each family also has a different income. Which families pay too much of their income for housing?

Family Name	Monthly Income	Monthly Rent	Monthly Mortgage Payment
Northrop	$2,100	$ 820	–
Garcia	$4,200	–	$1,675
Lee	$3,100	–	$ 900
Jackson	$3,875	$1,062	–

The Northrops and the Garcias pay too much of their income on housing, even though the Northrops' income is the least and the Garcias' is the greatest. In this chapter, you will learn how these families should decide how much they can afford to spend on housing.

◀9•1 Finding Affordable Housing

Jake earns $1,200 per month. He is looking for an apartment to rent. He sees the following ad in the newspaper.

Apartment for rent

1 bedroom/1 bathroom
All utilities included
$450 per month

Call Mr. Alonzo, 555-2468.

Should Jake consider renting this apartment?

New Idea

To live on someone else's property, you must pay the owner **rent** (rehnt), a monthly payment for the use of a house or an apartment. To buy your own house or condominium, most of the time you need a loan, or a **mortgage** (MAWR-gihj). To repay the bank and reduce the loan, a **mortgage payment** (MAWR-gihj PAY-muhnt) is made each month. Other monthly expenses can include **utilities** (yoo-TIHL-uh-teez), the costs for services such as natural gas, water, and electricity. As a general rule, your monthly housing expenses should be no more than 30% of your monthly income.

Example: Find the highest rent Jake can afford.

$1,200 × 0.30 = $360   ← 30% of his monthly salary

The $450 monthly rent is $90 more than Jake should pay, so he should look for another apartment.

Focus on the Idea

Housing expenses should not be more than 30% of monthly income.

Practice

Complete the following chart by finding the highest affordable monthly rent for each salary. The first one is done for you.

Monthly Income	Highest Affordable Rent
1. $1,450	$1,450 × 0.30 = $435
2. $2,200	_____
3. $1,750	_____
4. $3,000	_____

Apply the Idea

5. The next day Jake saw this ad in the newspaper.

   a. How much would Jake have to pay each month if he lives in the apartment with Jorge? _____

   b. Can he afford to share the apartment with Jorge? _____

Roommate wanted
to share expenses

2 bedrooms, utilities included
Your share: $650 per month

Call Jorge, 555-9753.

---

6. What would your share of the rent be if you had two roommates and the rent was $1,260 per month? _____

7. What is the highest mortgage payment you could afford each month if you earned $25,200 per year? _____

8. If you earned $22,000 per year, could you afford to pay $600 per month for rent? Why or why not?

   _____

Write About It

9. Do you agree with the rule that housing expenses should not be greater than 30% of income? If not, what percentage do you think is reasonable? Explain.

   _____

   _____

   _____

9•2 Calculating the Cost of Utilities

Frank pays for the utilities for his apartment. He has natural gas heat, and his gas bill is about half as much in summer as in winter. However, his electric bill, which includes air-conditioning, is about one third higher in summer than in winter. If Frank pays an average of $121 per month for gas and $29 per month for electricity in winter, how can he estimate the cost for these utilities in the summer?

New Idea

Bills for utilities, such as natural gas and electricity, are usually paid monthly. The costs for these utilities vary by month and season. For budgeting purposes, it is important to be able to predict the approximate amounts of these bills. One way to do this is to use the **average** monthly cost of the utilities. (See Lesson 3•1.) Then estimate the approximate cost per month.

Example: Estimate Frank's monthly cost for utilities in the summer.

Frank can use his winter bills to estimate the bills for each summer month:

$\frac{\$121}{2}$ is about $\frac{\$120}{2} = \$60$ ← Estimated cost of gas

Now estimate $\frac{1}{3}$ of the winter electric bill.

$\frac{\$29}{3}$ is about $\frac{\$30}{3} = \$10$

Then add $10 to the monthly winter electric bills.

$29 + $10 is about $30 + $10 = $40

Add both estimates.

$60 + $40 = $100

Frank should budget about $100 for utilities each month in the summer.

Focus on the Idea

Since utility bills change each month, estimate to determine approximate monthly costs.

Practice

Estimate the totals for the following utility bills. Show your work for each. The first one is done for you.

1. If a natural gas bill is for $89 and an electric bill is for $47, what is the estimated total? _____ $90 + 50 = $140 _____

2. The April electric bill is $97. The bill for May is usually about one-fourth higher. How much is the estimated bill for May? _____

3. A September electric bill is usually one-third lower than an August bill. One August electric bill was $86. Estimate the amount of the September bill. _____

4. Gas cost $108 per month for January, February, and March. The electric bill was $37 for each of these months. What was the approximate total amount for utilities for the three months? _____

Apply the Idea

5. Gerry wants to put enough money aside to pay all of his July and August utility bills. His summer gas bills are usually about half of his winter bills. His winter gas bills average $142 per month. His electric bills are about $26 higher each month in summer than in winter. His winter electric bills average $52 per month. About how much should Gerry put aside to pay his July and August utility bills? _____

6. Hunter pays his gas bills on the budget plan. This means that the gas company bills him each month for one twelfth of the yearly amount. His monthly budget plan bill is $107. He puts this amount aside to pay his bill each month. Hunter estimated his yearly gas bill to be $1,200. Will he have enough? Explain why or why not.

_____

Write About It

7. What are some other ways you might be able to get an estimate for your monthly utility bills?

_____

_____

_____

◀9•3 Signing a Lease

Manuel has found an apartment. He must read the lease to determine how much he will have to pay before moving in. Here are some details:

- 1-Year Lease beginning February 1
- Rent (due first day of each month): $550
- Tenant will pay: electricity
- Landlord will pay: gas and water
- Security deposit: $1\frac{1}{2}$ months' rent

New Idea

Usually, a person who rents must sign a lease for an apartment or other housing. A **lease** (lees) is a contract that states the terms of agreement between a tenant and a landlord. The **tenant** (TEHN-uhnt) is the person renting the property, and the **landlord** (LAND-lawrd) is the owner of the property. The lease usually states the amount of the rent, when the rent is due, and the utilities for which the tenant and landlord are each responsible. A lease can be for any length of time, but generally is for one year.

A landlord may ask the tenant for a **security deposit** (sih-KYOOR-uh-tee dee-PAHZ-iht), which is an amount of money held by the landlord to cover any damage the tenant may cause to the property. The security deposit is refunded to the tenant (usually with interest) when the tenant moves out, after payment for damage, if any, is deducted.

Example: How much will Manuel have to pay before he moves into his new apartment?

Manuel will owe the landlord the rent for February, plus $1\frac{1}{2}$ months' rent for the security deposit.

Rent for February: $550
Security deposit: $\underline{+\ 825}$ ($550 × 1.5)
Total $1,375

Manuel will have to pay $1,375 on February 1.

Focus on the Idea

Determine from a lease how much you will have to pay before moving into an apartment and which utilities you will have to pay for.

Practice

Write the amount of each security deposit. Then find the total amount needed to move in, including the first month's rent. The first one is done for you.

1. Rent: $650 per month

   Security deposit: 2 months' rent

   a. Amount of security deposit: $\underline{\$650 \times 2 = \$1,300}$

   b. Total amount needed to move in: $\underline{\$1,300 + \$650 = \$1,950}$

2. Rent: $780 per month

   Security deposit: $1\frac{1}{2}$ months' rent

   a. Amount of security deposit: _____

   b. Total amount needed to move in: _____

3. Rent: $675 per month

   Security deposit: 2 months' rent

   a. Amount of security deposit: _____

   b. Total amount needed to move in: _____

Apply the Idea

4. Together, Terry and her roommate have $3,000 with which to move into an apartment. The rent is $825 a month and the security deposit is 2 months' rent. How much will they have left for moving expenses? _____

Write About It

5. Besides rent and utilities, what are some other requirements that might be in a lease?

   _____

   _____

   _____

9•4 Painting and Carpeting Your Home

IN THIS LESSON, YOU WILL LEARN
To calculate amounts of paint and carpet needed to calculate the costs of painting and carpeting

WORDS TO LEARN
Area *measure of a flat, enclosed region*
Dimensions *measurements of length of sides*
Square foot *a unit of measure for the area of a region that is 1 foot long and 1 foot wide*

Marla wants to paint the four walls and ceiling of her bedroom, but she doesn't know how much paint she will need. The label on the paint can says that one gallon of paint can cover up to 200 square feet. Marla decides to measure her room to see how many gallons of paint she will need.

New Idea

Before painting a wall or carpeting a floor, it is necessary to know the **area** (AIR-ee-uh), which is the measure of the flat region, that needs to be covered. To find the area of a rectangular region, first find the region's **dimensions** (duh-MEHN-shuhns), the length and the width, and then multiply. The product is usually expressed in square feet (ft^2). One **square foot** (skwair foot) is the area of a region that measures one foot long and one foot wide.

Examples: Marla's bedroom is 15 feet long and 12 feet wide. How much carpeting will she need?

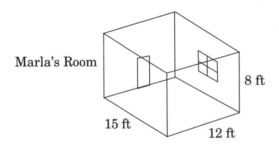

Marla's Room

15 ft   12 ft   8 ft

To find how much carpeting she will need, Marla needs to find the area of the floor. Marla's room is rectangular.

Area = length × width

Area = 15 feet × 12 feet

Area = 180 square feet (180 ft^2)

Marla will need 180 ft^2 of carpeting.

Marla also wants to paint the walls and ceiling of her bedroom. The ceiling is 8 feet high. How many gallons of paint will she need?

Marla needs to find the total area to be painted:

each long wall: 15 ft × 8 ft = 120 ft^2

both long walls: 120 ft^2 × 2 = 240 ft^2

each short wall: 12 ft × 8 ft = 96 ft^2

both short walls: 96 ft^2 × 2 = 192 ft^2

ceiling: 15 ft × 12 ft = 180 ft^2

Total area to be painted:
240 + 192 + 180 = 612 ft^2

To find the number of gallons of paint she needs, Marla divides:

$$\frac{\text{(total area to be painted)}}{\text{(area covered by one gallon)}} = \frac{612}{200} = 3.06 \text{ gallons}$$

Marla will need 3.06 gallons of paint.

✓Check the Math

1. If the paint Marla wants for her bedroom is sold only in gallons, how many gallons will she have to buy?

   _____

2. Alex wants to carpet his living room. The room is 20 feet long and 16 feet wide. Alex ordered 36 square feet of carpeting. Is this the correct amount of carpeting? Explain your answer.

   _____

◤Focus on the Idea

To find the area of a rectangular region, multiply length times width. The area of a floor determines the amount of carpeting needed. To find an amount of paint needed, divide the total area to be covered by the area each gallon will cover.

Practice

Find the area to be covered and the number of gallons of paint needed to cover the walls and ceiling of each room. (Assume that paint can be bought only in full gallons. One gallon of paint covers 200 square feet.) The first one is done for you.

	Room Dimensions	Ceiling Height	Area to Be Covered	Number of Gallons
3.	18 ft by 21 ft	9 ft	$(18 \times 9) \times 2 = 324$ $(21 \times 9) \times 2 = 378$ $18 \times 21 = 378$ $324 + 378 + 378 = 1{,}080 \text{ ft}^2$	$1{,}080 \div 200 = 5.4$ gal Must buy 6 gal.
4.	9 ft by 12 ft	8 ft		
5.	10 ft by 16 ft	8.5 ft		
6.	13 ft by 15 ft	8 ft		

Extend the Idea

Carpeting is usually sold by the square yard. A square yard has dimensions of 1 yard × 1 yard. Since 1 yard = 3 feet, 1 square yard = 3 feet × 3 feet = 9 square feet. So $1 \text{ yd}^2 = 9 \text{ ft}^2$. To change square feet to square yards, divide by 9.

Example: The carpeting Marla likes sells for $17.99 per square yard. How much will it cost to carpet her bedroom?

Marla knows that she needs 180 square feet of carpeting. Change 180 square feet to square yards.

$$180 \text{ ft}^2 \div 9 = 20 \text{ yd}^2$$

To find the total cost, multiply.

$$20 \text{ yd}^2 \times \$17.99 \text{ per square yard} = \$359.80$$

It will cost $359.80 to carpet Marla's bedroom.

7. How much will it cost Marla if she uses the same carpeting in her living room, which measures 13 feet by 18 feet?

_____

Practice

Find the cost of carpeting each room with carpet that costs $12 per square yard. The first one is done for you.

8. Living room: 12 ft by 24 ft

12 ft × 24 ft = 288 ft²

288 ft² ÷ 9 = 32 yd²

32 yd² × $12 = $384

9. Bedroom: 4.5 yd by 6 yd

10. Dining room: 11.7 ft by 15 ft

11. Bedroom: 12 ft by 14 ft

Apply the Idea

12. Patrick has a one-room apartment. The floor measures 20 feet by 30 feet, and the ceiling is 8.5 feet high. Patrick wants to paint the four walls with light blue paint that costs $13.99 per gallon. He wants to paint the ceiling with white paint that costs $9.99 per gallon. Each gallon of paint can cover up to 180 square feet. Both colors are sold only in gallons.

a. How many gallons of light blue paint should Patrick buy?

_____

b. How many gallons of ceiling paint should he buy?

_____

c. How much will he spend in all on paint? _____

13. The diagram shows the dimensions of Anne's bedroom floor. She plans to paint a 3-foot-wide red border around the floor. What size area rug should she buy to cover the center of her floor, as shown on the diagram? _____

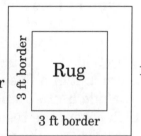

✏ Write About It

14. Why do you divide by 3 to change feet to yards but divide by 9 to change square feet to square yards?

_____

_____

◀9•5 Calculating Fixed Monthly Home Expenses

Charles and Shenequa are planning to buy a house. They have $30,000 for a down payment. They have found a house that they like. The house costs $140,000, and the current annual interest rate is 8.75%.

↶Remember

Interest is what the bank charges a borrower for the use of the bank's money. A mortgage is a loan obtained from a bank for the purchase of a house or condominium.

New Idea

For a major purchase, such as a house, the buyer usually does not pay the entire amount in one single payment. Instead, the buyer makes a **down payment** (down PAY-muhnt) by paying a small part of the purchase price and then takes out a mortgage to borrow the rest of the money. The mortgage payment is a **fixed expense** (fihkst ehk-SPENS) of owning a residence. A fixed expense is a payment you make each month. The amount of a fixed expense stays the same. Other expenses might include **homeowner's insurance** (HOHM-oh-nirz ihn-SHOOR-uhns), which covers the residence and the owner's belongings, and a **property tax** (PRAHP-uhr-tee taks), a payment that is based on the value of a residence and the land it is built on.

The following chart shows the monthly mortgage payment per $1,000 for various interest rates and time periods.

Monthly Mortgage Payments per $1,000

Years of Mortgage	Annual Interest Rates			
	8.5%	8.75%	9%	9.75%
15	$9.85	$10	$10.15	$10.60
20	8.68	8.84	9	9.49
25	8.06	8.23	8.40	8.92
30	7.69	7.87	8.05	8.60

To calculate your monthly mortgage payment, find the number of years of your mortgage and your annual interest rate in the chart. Multiply that number by the number of thousands of dollars you will borrow.

Example: If Charles and Shenequa take out a 30-year mortgage, how much will their monthly mortgage payment be?

They will need to borrow $110,000, after making a down payment of $30,000. From the chart, for 30 years at 8.75% annual interest, they will have to pay $7.87 for every $1,000 borrowed. Since they borrowed $110,000, multiply $7.87 × 110 = $865.70.

Their monthly mortgage payment will be $865.70.

✓Check Your Understanding

1. Suppose that Charles and Shenequa could have made a down payment of $35,000 and borrowed $105,000 for 15 years at 8.75% annual interest. Would their monthly payments be less for the 15-year loan than for the 30-year loan on $110,000? Why or why not?

◀ Focus on the Idea

Buying a house involves a number of payments. To calculate a monthly mortgage payment, find the amount for the length of the mortgage and the annual interest rate in the monthly mortgage payment chart. Multiply that amount by the number of thousands of dollars that will be borrowed.

Practice

Find the monthly mortgage payment for each amount borrowed. The first one is done for you.

	Amount to Borrow	Number of Years	Annual Interest Rate	Monthly Mortgage Payment
2.	$100,000	20	9.75%	$9.49 × 100 = $949
3.	$85,000	15	8.75%	
4.	$193,000	25	8.5%	
5.	$205,000	30	9.75%	

Extend the Idea

There are many other expenses to consider when you own a house or condominium. Two of these are homeowner's insurance and property taxes. Often, these expenses are not paid monthly, but annually or semi-annually. You can figure out the monthly expense for each of these by dividing the annual amount by 12.

Example: Charles and Shenequa bought homeowner's insurance, which costs them $550 per year. The property tax on their house and land is $3,090 per year. Including their mortgage payment, how much are their monthly expenses?

Since the costs are given per year, you need to divide these amounts by 12 to find the monthly costs.

Homeowner's insurance:
$550 ÷ 12 = $45.83 per month

Property tax:
$3,090 ÷ 12 = $257.50 per month

To find their total monthly expenses, add:

Mortgage payment:	$ 865.70
Homeowner's insurance:	45.83
Property tax:	+ 257.50
Monthly expenses:	$1,169.03

Charles and Shenequa will have monthly expenses of $1,169.03.

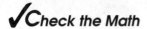

6. Juanita's mortgage payment on her condominium is $875 per month, her homeowner's insurance is $250 per year, and her property tax is $1,500 per year. Juanita computed her monthly expenses to be $2,625. What did she do wrong? What will her monthly expenses be? _____

Practice

Find the monthly expenses for each situation in the chart. The first one is done for you.

	Monthly Mortgage Payment	Homeowner's Insurance (Annual)	Property Taxes Per Year	Monthly House Expenses
7.	$1,245	$750	$4,200	$1,657.50
8.	$982	$450	$1,900	_____
9.	$695	$380	$1,400	_____

Apply the Idea

10. Mel wants to buy a house that costs $205,500. He has $45,000 for a down payment, and will take out a mortgage to pay for the rest. Mortgage interest rates are at 8.75% per year. Based on the monthly mortgage payment chart, what is the least amount he can pay each month for this house?

    _____

11. The Changs need to borrow $121,000 for a house. One bank will give them a mortgage for 25 years at 8.75% per year. Another bank will lend them the same amount for 30 years at 9% per year.

    a. What is the amount of difference in monthly payments between the two bank plans? _____

    b. What is the amount of difference between the two plans over the life of the mortgage? (Hint: the life of the mortgage is the total number of monthly payments needed to pay back the entire loan. The life of a 30-year mortgage is 30 × 12 = 360 payments.) _____

Write About It

12. What are some of the trends, or relationships, that you notice in the monthly mortgage payment chart?

    _____

    _____

Chapter 9   Review

In This Chapter, You Have Learned

- To compare housing and determine the affordable choice
- To estimate monthly utility bills
- To calculate apartment expenses based on a lease
- To calculate amount and cost of painting and carpeting
- To calculate monthly expenses of owning a house

Words You Know

From the lists of "Words to Learn," choose the word or phrase that best completes each statement.

1. I pay for electricity, but my landlord pays for my other
   _____ .

2. The landlord asked the _____ in Apartment 102 to pay the rent on time.

3. The _____ of my bedroom are 15 feet by 18 feet.

4. I borrowed money to buy my home, so now each month I send the bank a check to pay off my _____ .

5. I signed a one-year _____ that states that I will pay $770 a month for this apartment.

6. This gallon of paint covers a(n) _____ of 180 square feet.

More Practice

What is the highest affordable rent based on each of the following incomes? (Rent should be no more than 30% of income.)

7. Monthly Income: $1,240
   Highest Affordable Rent: _____ per month

8. Yearly Income: $19,580
   Highest Affordable Rent: _____ per month

Estimate the total amount paid for the given utilities.

9. **Apartment A.** gas: $78; electricity: $31; hot water: $18
   Estimated Total: _____

10. **Apartment B.** gas: $124; electricity: $59.75
    Estimated Total: _____

Write the amount of each security deposit.

11. Rent: $825 per month
    Security deposit: 2 months' rent
    Amount of security deposit: _____

12. Rent: $675 per month

Security deposit: $1\frac{1}{2}$ months' rent

Amount of security deposit: _____

Express the area of each room in square feet.

13. 12 ft by 13 ft

Area: _____

14. 5 yd by 3 yd

Area: _____

Express the area of each room in square yards.

15. 4.4 yd by 3.8 yd

Area: _____

16. 18 ft by 21 ft

Area: _____

Use the monthly mortgage payment chart on page 159 to complete exercises 17 and 18.

	Amount to Borrow	Years of Mortgage	Annual Interest Rate	Monthly Mortgage Payment
17.	$110,000	25	9.75%	_____
18.	$77,000	30	8.75%	_____

Problems You Can Solve

19. Mr. and Mrs. Walters plan to move to a new apartment. Mr. Walters earns $32,000 per year. Mrs. Walters earns $3,600 per month. They have decided that they will pay no more than 30% of their combined salaries for rent. What is the highest affordable rent they can pay? _____

20. Jason signed a one-year lease to rent an apartment for $815.50 per month. He will be sharing the apartment with a roommate. If the landlord requires $1\frac{1}{2}$ months' security deposit, what is Jason's share of the first month's rent plus security deposit? _____

21. For Your Portfolio Work together with a partner. Look through the classified ads in a newspaper. Assume you and your partner have 20% of the purchase price needed for the down payment on a house. Find a house you would like to buy and research the current rates for a mortgage for 30 years. Present your findings to the class. Determine what your monthly mortgage payments would be for that house.

_____

_____

_____

Chapter 9   Practice Test

If rents should be no more than 30% of income, what is the highest rent affordable based on each of the following incomes?

1. Monthly Income: $2,220
   Highest Affordable Rent: _____ per month

2. Yearly Income: $25,590
   Highest Affordable Rent: _____ per month

Estimate the total amount paid for the given utilities. Then find the exact total.

3. Gas: $102, electricity: $39.95, water: $11

   Estimated Total: _____

   Exact Total: _____

Write the amount of each security deposit.

4. Rent: $915 per month
   Security deposit: 2 months' rent
   Amount of deposit: _____

5. Rent: $465 per month
   Security deposit: $1\frac{1}{2}$ months' rent
   Amount of deposit: _____

Express the area of each room in square feet.

6. 14 ft by 16 ft bedroom
   Area: _____

7. 3 yd by 4 yd living room
   Area: _____

Use the monthly mortgage payment chart on page 159 to complete exercises 8 and 9.

	Amount to Borrow	Years of Mortgage	Annual Interest Rate	Monthly Mortgage Payment
8.	$120,000	20	9.75%	_____
9.	$96,000	30	8.50%	_____

10. Rod must decide if he will share an apartment with a friend. Rod earns $1,400 per month. His friend works part-time and earns $550 per month. Neither of them will pay more than 30% of his income on rent.

    a. How much rent can Rod afford to pay on his own?

    _____

    b. How much rent can Rod and his friend afford if they move in together? _____

    c. Do you think that it would be fair for Rod to share an apartment with this friend? Why or why not?

    _____

    _____

Glossary

A

Account balance amount available in an account (4•1)

Adjust fix or change by reducing or increasing (3•5)

Amount of discount how much is subtracted from the regular price (5•2)

Apply to make a request in writing or in person (1•6)

Area the measure of a flat, enclosed region (9•4)

Arrival time a specified time that a bus or train comes to a place (8•1)

Available funds income remaining after all expenses have been paid (4•7)

Average the typical value of a group of numbers (3•1)

B

Balanced budget a budget based on an income that is at least as much as the expenses (3•4)

Bank statement a report of all transactions and the balance in an account (4•2)

Best buy the highest quality of merchandise or service available for the least amount of money (5•4)

Better buy the item that gives you more for less money (7•2)

Board the expenses for meals (3•2)

Bonus an extra item included with a purchase at no additional cost (5•4)

Budget a plan for how to spend money (3•3)

C

Calories units for measuring the energy-producing value in foods (7•1)

Cap the highest interest rate that can be charged on a variable loan (4•6)

Car insurance an agreement in which an insurance company promises to pay your expenses in case of a car accident or theft (8•4)

Change the amount of money that is the difference between the cost of an item and the amount used to pay (6•2)

Charge to buy an item now, then pay for it later (6•4)

Charge account a credit account issued by a store that allows a person to charge purchases (6•4)

Check register a personal record of checking account activity (4•1)

Claim a request you make of your insurance company telling them about an accident or theft and asking them to pay for it (8•4)

Closing balance the amount in an account at the end date of a bank statement (4•2)

Collision insurance insurance that covers damage to your car (8•4)

Commuter a person who takes public or private transportation to and from work (8•2)

Commuting traveling back and forth to work or school on a regular basis (8•2)

Compound interest interest paid on both the principal and the accumulated interest (4•5)

Comprehensive insurance insurance that covers damage to your car when the car is unoccupied (8•4)

Credit card account a credit account issued by a bank that allows a person to charge purchases (6•4)

D

Debt money owed that must be repaid, or an amount spent beyond the income (3•4)

Deductible the amount a person must pay before the insurance company begins to pay (8•4)

Departure time a specified time that a bus or train leaves a place (8•1)

Deposit to put money into a checking account or savings account (4•1)

Deposit a partial payment for an item that holds, or reserves, that item for the customer (6•3)

Destination the place where you want to be when you complete your trip (8•2)

Dimensions measurements of length of sides (9•4)

Down payment the amount of money paid toward the purchase price of an item (8•3)

Down payment the amount a buyer pays before borrowing the rest of the money to make a purchase (9•5)

E

Earnings money paid for work performed; also called wages, or salary (1•2)

Earnings statement a stub attached to a paycheck that lists gross pay, deductions, and net pay (2•1)

Employees people who work for someone in return for wages or salary (1•5)

Employee benefit a service an employer provides to its employees (2•2)

Employer a person who hires and pays workers (1•5)

Expense the cost of something you bought, rented, or otherwise paid for (3•1)

F

FICA/Medicare the money paid to government agencies for Social Security and medical insurance (2•1)

Fixed expense a cost or charge that stays the same every month (9•5)

Fixed expenses expenses that remain the same over a period of time (3•2)

Fixed interest rate a rate of interest that does not change for the length of the loan (4•6)

Full-time job a job that requires from 35 to 40 hours of work each week (1•3)

G

Gross pay the total earnings before deductions are subtracted (2•1)

H

Hidden cost the cost of something you need to have in order to use another item (5•1)

Homeowner's insurance the insurance on a house and the owner's belongings (9•5)

Hourly wage amount paid for each hour of work (1•3)

I

Income tax the money paid to the government based on the amount of money earned (2•4)

Ingredients food or food products used in a recipe (7•4)

Installment plan a sales method whereby a customer makes repeated payments of equal amounts over a definite time period until the total cost is paid (6•3)

Interest money the bank pays to you based on the amount of money in your savings account (4•3)

Interest the fee charged by a bank for taking out a loan (8•3)

J

Job-related expenses expenses that are necessary in order to perform a job (1•2)

L

Landlord a property owner (9•3)

Layaway plan a sales method whereby a store saves an item on which the customer makes a deposit until the customer has paid the total cost over a specific period of time (6•3)

Lease a legal contract that states the tenant's and landlord's responsibilities regarding an apartment (9•3)

Leisure activities activities done for fun (3•3)

Liability insurance insurance that pays for bodily injury and property damage for other people if you are responsible for an accident (8•4)

Limit the greatest number of items that a shopper is allowed to buy at the sale price (5•4)

Loan money borrowed (4•6)

M

Manufacturer's coupon cents-off coupon that can be used in any store that sells a certain product (7•3)

Merchandise the products for sale (5•3)

Mortgage a loan to buy a house or condominium (9•1)

Mortgage payment the monthly payment to a bank to reduce the amount of a loan (9•1)

N

Net pay the amount of salary that remains after all deductions have been subtracted from gross pay (2•1)

Non-taxable item an item on which no sales tax is collected (6•1)

Nutrients the useful parts of food that the body needs for growth (7•1)

O

Opening balance the amount in an account at the beginning date of a statement (4•2)

Overdrawn account an account on which a check is written for more money than the account balance (4•2)

Overtime number of hours worked beyond a regular full-time work week (1•3)

P

Part-time job a job that requires fewer working hours than an full-time week (1•1)

Passbook the record that shows savings account transactions (4•3)

Payment plan a method of paying for items purchased by using either an installment plan, a layaway plan, or a credit card (6•5)

Payroll deductions the amounts subtracted from gross pay (2•1)

Premium your cost for insurance for a given period of time (8•4)

Principal total amount of money on which interest is paid (4•4)

Property tax a tax based on the value of a residence and the land it is located on (9•5)

Proportion a statement that two ratios are equal (7•4)

Purchase price total of all costs for an item, including sales tax (6•1)

Q

Quarterly every 3 months, or 4 times per year (4•5)

R

Rate price for a given quantity of an item (7•2)

Rate of discount a fraction or a percent of the regular price (5•2)

Ratio a comparison of two numbers (7•2)

Rebate money given back to the customer by the manufacturer (8•3)

Recipe instructions for making a food dish (7•4)

Reconcile to match the information in the check register with the transactions shown for the account on the bank statement (4•2)

Refund the money returned by the government if income tax deductions are too high (2•5)

Regular price the price of a item as suggested by the manufacturer (5•1)

Rent the money paid for housing in someone else's property (9•1)

Round-trip a trip to a place and back, usually over the same route (8•2)

S

Salary an amount of money paid by an employer for work performed (1•2)

Sale price the price of an item at less than the regular price (5•2)

Sales tax a percentage charge added to the price of goods or services purchased (6•1)

Savings account a bank account on which interest is paid (4•3)

Schedule a list of arrival and departure times for a train or bus (8•1)

Security deposit the tenant's money held by a landlord to cover any damages that the tenant might cause (9•3)

Shipping and handling charges the costs added to the merchandise total for taking an order and mailing it (5•3)

Simple interest interest paid at the end of a time period (usually a year) (4•4)

Square foot a unit of measure for the area of a region that is 1 foot long and 1 foot wide (9•4)

Standard deduction the amount of income that will not be taxed (2•5)

Store coupon cents-off coupon that can be used only in particular stores (7•3)

T

Take-home pay the net pay, or the amount of salary that remains after all deductions have been subtracted from gross pay (2•3)

Taxes the amounts of money paid to the local, state, and/or federal governments (2•1)

Tax table a chart that lists the amount of tax that must be paid according to income and marital status (2•4)

Taxable item an item on which a sales tax is charged (6•1)

Tenant a person who rents an apartment or other housing (9•3)

Time card a card used for recording the number of hours a person works (1•4)

Total cost the regular price of an item plus any hidden costs (5•1)

Transaction any activity in an account that changes the balance (4•1)

U

Uninsured motorist insurance insurance that pays your damages caused by an uninsured driver (8•4)

Unit price the cost of one unit of an item (7•2)

Unpaid balance the amount owed on a credit card account or store charge account (6•4)

Utilities services such as natural gas, water, and electricity (9•1)

V

Variable expenses expenses that may change from one time period to the next (3•2)

Variable interest rate a rate of interest that changes or varies during the loan period (4•6)

W

W-2 form a record of an employee's total payroll deductions for the year (2•4)

Wages the amount of money a worker earns in a given time period (1•1)

Withdrawal amount taken out of an account (4•1)

Answers

Chapter 1   Earning Money

1•1   Keeping Track of Part-Time Wages

1. $61.25
3. $61.25
5. a. Rita
   b. $4.75
7. Yes, add the wages of all the workers and compare the total to $300.

1•2   Deducting Job-Related Expenses from Earnings

1. Answer should include the fact that she must pay for the expenses. The money comes out of her salary; it is not added to her salary.
3. $146.30; $1,353.70
5. $39.00
7. $317.25
9. $29,647.00
11. a. Yes
    b. Transportation costs: $4.25 × 3 or $12.75,
    $12.75 + $2.50 = $15.25.
    $150 − $15.25 = $134.75,
    which is greater than $125.

1•3   Figuring Hourly Wages and Overtime

1. a. Multiply $18.50 by 35.
   b. $647.50
3. $444.00
5. $691.25
7. $740; $906.50
9. $411.25; $587.55
11. $14.25
13. $606.00
15. The nurse's aide earns more for a full-time week. She earns $6.80 × 36 = $244.80. The clerk earns $6.00 × 40 = $240.00.

1•4   Keeping a Weekly Time Card

1. 7 hours
3. 9 P.M. to 12 A.M. (midnight) is 3 hours, 12 A.M. to 4 A.M. is 4 hours, less 1 hour for a break
5. $11\frac{1}{4}$ hours
7. $5\frac{1}{2}$ hours
9. $232.50

1•5   Working with Hourly Rates and Tips

1. c
3. $184.32; $184.32
5. $237.00; $685.00
7. $13.25

1•6   Computing a Salary From Information Given in a Want Ad

1. Possible answer: Multiply 3 × 15, then divide 110.25 by 15.
3. $448.80
5. $7.50
7. $297.50
9. $23,400.00; $1,950.00
11. $560.00; $2,425.00
13. $18.87; $301.85; $15,696
15. $6.90
17. $10.47or more per hour

Chapter 1 Review

1. e
2. d
3. b
4. a
5. c
6. Hannah
7. $216.00
8. $285.25
9. $367.50
10. $636.00
11. $8\frac{3}{4}$ hours
12. $9\frac{1}{4}$ hours
13. $23,424
14. $558.65
15. $270
16. Nurse's Aide; $8,910

Chapter 2   Take-Home Pay

2•1   Understanding Earnings Statements

1. The amount of money paid to the U.S. government
3. Salary remaining after all deductions are subtracted
5. $55.69
7. 24
9. Each employee's salary and the number of dependents varies.

2•2   Calculating Deductions

1. Maria
3. $290.87
5. $111.88
7. Hector and Kim
9. $23,271.04

2•3   Calculating Take-Home Pay

1. Add the deductions.
3. Subtract the total deductions from the gross pay.
5. $1,001.00
7. $12,012.00
9. No. Her check should have been for $1,114.37. $1,601.37 represents her gross pay with the total for her deductions added instead of subtracted.

2•4   Understanding Tax Forms

1. $16,765.43
3. His yearly deduction for Social Security was $1,039.46.
5. $1,504

2•5   Filling Out Tax Forms

1. No, the tax table increases for every $50. Jose's taxable income is $10,565.43, so his taxes are $1,586, or $7 more than Mark's.
3. On line 3 of his W-2 form
5. Line 10
7. Possible answer: If the tax you owe is more than the tax withheld, you owe money; if the tax withheld is more, you will receive a refund.
9. $1,504
11. Yes

Chapter 2 Review

1. deduction
2. Net pay
3. tax
4. employee benefits
5. A W-2 form
6. standard deduction
7. city tax
8. $16,724.03
9. $1,690.72
10. Adjusted gross income
11. Line 1
12. Total wages, salaries and tips
13. $15,906.00
14. $122.05
15. $227.14
16. $872.86
17. No, Mary owes an additional $90.00 in Federal Taxes
18. $1,083.38

Chapter 3 Budgeting

3•1 Finding Average Monthly Expenses

1. Matt's answer is not very reasonable. First total Matt's estimated expenses, $400 + $600 = $1,500. $1,500 ÷ 3 = $500.
3. Add: $625 + $135 + $290 = $1,050. Then divide by 3: $1,050 ÷ 3 = $350.
5. $430; $435
7. $1,270
9. If your calculated answer is near your estimate, then your calculated response may be correct.

3•2 Average Fixed and Variable Expenses

1. Rent, life insurance
3. $500
5. $330
7. a. $87.50
   b. $53.13

3•3 Making a Monthly Budget

1. This would reduce his monthly expenses by about $60. However, you do not know if this will reduce Bill's monthly expenses enough because you do not know what his monthly expenses are.
3. a. Fixed expense
   b. $86.00
5. $537.50
7. $1,389.00
9. Approximately $9.30

3•4 Using a Budget

1. Yes
3. Yes
5. $271
7. Students' work should show a budget which includes all of Greg's expenses.

3•5 Adjusting a Budget

1. −$20 and −$30
3. $1,075
5. $64.50
7. Nick would have $30 available to put into savings each month.

Chapter 3 Review

1. Fixed expenses
2. Debt
3. Budget
4. Balanced
5. Adjust
6. $1,000; $991; $247.75
7. $1,400; $1,426; $356.50
8. Rent and life insurance
9. $515.50
10. $173.08
11. $1,031; Rent; $625; Gasoline; $80; Groceries; $160; Electricity; $48; Leisure Activities; $80. Savings may be $40 or more; Total Expenses, depending on savings, should be $1,033 or more.
12–14. Answers will vary according to chosen variable expenses. The total of these three variable expenses should be between $0 and $175 so that the total expenses are less than or equal to Joe's income.
15. Answer must be less than or equal to $335.
16. $50
17. Answers will vary. However, income must be changed to $928, rent must be changed to $475, and $150 must be cut from variable expenses.

Chapter 4 Personal Banking

4•1 Managing a Checking Account

1. Greg needed to make the deposit before writing his check. Otherwise he would not have had enough money in his account to write the check for the insurance.
3. $8.55
5. Jaime is incorrect. Because his balance is less than $1,000, the Farmers Bank will charge him a service fee of $4.50.
7. $13.20
9. $473.35
11. $66.50
13. March 5; 560; Natural Gas Co.; _____ ; $51.78; $325.02
15. March 12; 561; Berger's Store; _____ ; $150.54; $299.23
17. $4.50

4•2 Reconciling a Bank Statement

1. Opening balance; $76.40
3. $223.90
5. $133.50
7. $1,375.15
9. $545.25
11. $341.45
13. $251.45
15. $301.45
17. $281.20
19. $178.80

4•3 Using a Savings Account

1. Every month
3. $450.00
5. The $0.45 interest was added.
7. $675.00
9. $345.00

4•4 Finding Simple Interest

1. 0.45
3. 0.01
5. 2.00
7. 0.054
9. 0.13
11. 0.0004
13. $13.46
15. $2.54
17. $1.12
19. $30.00
21. $30.66
23. $23.63
25. $30.00; $2.50

4•5 Finding Compound Interest

1. You would want to go to a bank that pays 3% annual interest compounded quarterly. For example, $1,000 compounded quarterly at an annual interest rate of 3% for one year equals $1,030.43. But $1,000 compounded annually at a simple interest rate of 3% for one year equals only $1,030.00. The interest rate compounded quarterly earns $0.43 more.
3. $601.92; $1.93; $601.92; $1.93; $603.85
5. $776.60
7. Yes, you should use 0.5 as the "time" in the interest formula since 6 months is half of a year.
9. b; $30.55
11. a; $143.15
13. $6.51

4•6   Borrowing Money

1. 17.6%
3. 25.75%
5. 15.5%

4•7   Comparing Loan Repayment Plans

1. $241.00
3. $105.50
5. $84; $1,484; $61.83
7. $1,562.50; $4,062.50; $67.71
9. Jamal could afford the interest plan. Jamal's available monthly funds are $111. The loan would cost him $73 each month.

Chapter 4 Review

1. c
2. g
3. b
4. h
5. e
6. f
7. a
8. d
9. $81.90
10. $135.35
11. $36.85
12. $149.60
13. $561.75
14. $189.49
15. $43.75
16. $52.50
17. $3.20; $3.20; $803.20
18. $803.20; $3.21; $803.20; $3.21; $806.41
19. 12%
20. 12.5%
21. $360; $1,860; $51.67
22. $531.25; $1,381.25; $23.02
23. $1,545.51
24. $9,780

Chapter 5   Becoming an Informed Shopper

5•1   Recognizing Hidden Costs

1. $40; $38.25
3. $73; $72.15

5•2   Understanding Discounts and Sales

1. No, $84 × 0.25 = $21 (amount of discount), $84 − $21 = $63 (sale price). Although Sports Center had the greatest rate of discount, the Hi Flyers are cheaper at both Skate City and Roller Madness.
3. $15.63; $109.37
5. $0.66; $11.34
7. $27.75; $157.25
9. 13%
11. 33%
13. 50%
15. 75%
17. $23.00
19. $38.80
21. $38 jeans; $34.20
23. $62.30

5•3   Shopping from Catalogs

1. Yes. He added in the $4.95 charge for shipping and handling.
3. $4.95; $39.94
5. $3.95; $28.95
7. $5.95; $11.85; $62.80
9. $6.95; $15.80; $85.50

5•4   Reading Advertisements

1. No. Since Moto Oil has a limit of one case per customer at the sale price, two cases cost Matt $18.99 + $24.99, or $43.98. Two cases of Super Oil would have cost $42.00 and two cases of Auto Oil would have cost $40.00. Thus, Auto Oil would have been the best buy.
3. $6.80
5. $18.48
7. $20.40
9. $57.00
11. Time limits: Mr. Drip Coffee Maker is on sale only through Saturday and Quick Start Coffee Machine is on sale only for 2 days.
13. $260
15. Wally's Warehouse; it has the less expensive price for a 27" TV on Saturday.
17. Wally's Warehouse; the price is less expensive for a 27" TV on Saturday.

Chapter 5 Review

1. merchandise
2. rate of discount; regular price
3. hidden costs
4. total cost
5. $52; $51.73
6. $68; $67.87
7. $11.20; $44.80
8. $41.83; $83.67
9. $2.93; $16.57
10. $4.50; $7.00; $50.45
11. $6.50; $5.50; $132.75
12. $18.00
13. $31.00
14. $18.00
15. $18.00
16. The radio from M&M Electronics is a better deal. Answers will vary according to chosen ads. Answer should include several ads for the same item. Students should choose which item is the best deal according to the content of the ad.

Chapter 6 Making a Purchase

6•1 Understanding and Calculating Sales Tax

1. Yes. Sales tax in Wyoming is 4%, so her total would be $49.91.
3. $1.16; $26.91
5. $131.25; $1,631.25
7. $1,271.43; $63.57; $1,335.00
9. $149.15
11. $79.32
13. $1,899.85
15. $4.88; $5.48; $.27; $10.63
17. a. $17,808
    b. $17,225
    c. $583

6•2 Estimating and Calculating Change

1. Possible answer: To be sure you have enough money
3. $90; $10; $10; $25; $135.00; $132.08
5. $3.00; $3.26
7. No. Possible answer: The number stored in memory should be the amount of her purchases, not the amount she gave the clerk.
9. $25.14
11. $75.00
13. $20
15. $10.47

6•3 Installment Buying

1. No. Leroy would pay $250, which is $4.05 more than the cost of the item.
3. $102.00
5. $360.00
7. $86.00
9. $180 × 0.10 = $18.00;
   $180 − $18 = $162;
   $162 × 3 = $54;
   $162 − $54 = $108
11. $95 × 0.10 = $9.50;
    $95 − $9.50 = $85.50;
    $85.50 ÷ 3 = $28.50
13. $79.25
15. $144.00
17. $47.96

6•4 Using Bank Credit Cards and Charge Accounts

1. 0.73%; 0.0073
3. 2.16%; 0.0216
5. 1.55%; $355.43
7. 0.8%; $806.40
9. $126.19

6•5 Reviewing Credit Plans

1. $165.00; $164.95
3. $275.00; $273.50
5. $453.00; $454.00; $452.25
7. a. $2.18
   b. Sally paid more by $2.07.

Chapter 6 Review

1. a
2. d
3. e
4. b
5. c
6. $7.50; $257.50
7. $1.13; $14.08
8. $3
9. $8
10. $42.70
11. $.80
12. $454.00
13. $1,530.00
14. $229.80
15. $84.00
16. 1.75%; $427.35
17. 0.62%; $223.56
18. 1.29%; $2,279.03
19. $44.59
20. a. $25.38
    b. Joel; $24.62

Chapter 7   Buying Food

7•1   Using Nutrition Labels

1. 75
3. 25
5. 150
7. 375

7•2   Using Unit Pricing to Compare Costs

1. Madison Variety Store
3. $\frac{\$3.99}{64}$; $.06 per ounce
5. $\frac{\$2.49}{3}$; $.83 per box
7. 16-ounce bag for $2.89; Possible answer: The unit cost of the 16-ounce bag is $.18 per ounce, compared to $.20 per ounce for the 12-ounce bag.

7•3   Using Coupons

1. $2.48
3. $3.07
5. $1.03

7•4   Preparing Meals

1. 8 cups
3. $2\frac{2}{3}$ cups
5. $2\frac{1}{2}$ cups
7. $1\frac{1}{2}$ cans of soup, $1\frac{1}{2}$ eggs, $\frac{3}{4}$ cup of bread crumbs
9. No. Possible answer: He should have used $\frac{1}{8}$ cup of olive oil and $\frac{3}{4}$ teaspoon of anchovy paste. The $\frac{1}{4}$ teaspoon of lemon juice is correct.

Chapter 7 Review

1. coupon
2. nutrients
3. ingredient
4. unit price
5. recipe
6. calorie
7. better buy
8. 210 calories
9. 35 calories
10. $4.33
11. $1.44
12. $3.67
13. $.40
14. $.46
15. $.12
16. $12.25
17. $15.12
18. $6.75
19. 39 ounces
20. $1\frac{1}{4}$ teaspoons
21. $6\frac{2}{3}$ scoops
22. The store brand. 3 pounds cost $5.07 compared to $5.11.

Chapter 8 Transportation

8•1 Using Public Transportation

1. 5:20 P.M.; 7:15 A.M.
3. 15 minutes; 6:32 P.M.
5. 7:33 A.M.

8•2 Calculating Commuting Costs

1. Yes, because he can subtract the $2.50 per day from $13.75. The daily cost will be $11.25 by train, which is less than $12 per day by bus.
3. $6.25
5. $11.67
7. Train A
9. $3.25
11. $5.90
13. $8.73 per round-trip

8•3 Buying an Automobile

1. Possible answer: No, because now he must pay interest on $8,050 rather than $7,300, since he cannot apply the rebate to the purchase price. The interest is now $8,050 × 0.125 = $1,006.25. This makes the total cost of the car now $10,050 + $1,006.25 − $750 = $10,306.25. Now the best way to buy the car is by using the 2.9% financing rather than the rebate.
3. $17,325
5. $22,341.75
7. $1185.92
9. $600.12 more
11. a. $14,784
    b. $284; $13,300

8•4 Insuring and Maintaining a Car

1. No. The insurance company would have paid $1,200 − $250 = $950 for the repairs.
3. $290; Basic Personal Injury
5. $250; Uninsured Motorist
7. $3,096; $258
9. $1,935; $161.25
11. $500
13. $244.50

Chapter 8 Review

1. c
2. d
3. b
4. a
5. a. 8:12 A.M.
   b. 8:48 A.M.
6. $5.17
7. $6.50
8. $9.53
9. $2.58
10. $14,822.50
11. $3,362; $280.17
12. $10,416.60
13. a. $870
    b. $500
14. $113.93 per month

Chapter 9   Housing

9•1   Finding Affordable Housing

1. $435
3. $525
5. **a.** $325
   b. yes
7. $630

9•2   Calculating the Cost of Utilities

1. $140
3. $30
5. $300

9•3   Signing a Lease

1. **a.** $1,300
   b. $1,950
3. **a.** $1,350
   b. $2,025

9•4   Painting and Carpeting Your Home

1. 4 gal
3. Area to be covered: 1,080 ft^2;
   Number of gallons: 6 gal
5. Area to be covered: 602 ft^2;
   Number of gallons: 4 gal
7. $467.74 to carpet her living room
9. $324
11. $224.04
13. 9×9 feet

9•5   Calculating Fixed Monthly Home Expenses

1. No. Possible answer: The monthly payment would be $1,050 rather than $865.70. Even though you are borrowing less money, you are paying it back in half the time. The payments over a shorter period are usually higher.
3. $850
5. $1,763
7. $1,657.50
9. $843.34
11. **a.** The monthly payment for the 30-year mortgage is $21.78 less.
    b. The 30-year mortgage will cost $51,909 more.

Chapter 9 Review

1. utilities
2. tenant
3. dimensions
4. mortgage
5. lease
6. area
7. $372
8. $489.50
9. $130
10. $184
11. $1,650
12. $1,012.50
13. 156 ft^2
14. 135 ft^2
15. 16.72 yd^2
16. 42 yd^2
17. $981.20
18. $605.99
19. $10,680
20. $1,019.38